Policing and Stress

❖

Policing and Stress

❖

HEITH COPES

Editor
University of Alabama—Birmingham

M. L. DANTZKER

Series Editor

PEARSON
Prentice
Hall

Upper Saddle River, New Jersey 07458

Library of Congress Cataloging-in-Publication Data

Policing and stress/Heith Copes, editor.
    p. cm.
    "Policing and . . . series."
    ISBN 0-13-112371-8
    1. Police—Job stress. I. Copes, Heith

HV7936.J63P65 2005
363.2'01'9—dc22

2004040018

Executive Editor: Frank Mortimer, Jr.
Assistant Editor: Korrine Dorsey
Marketing Manager: Tim Peyton
Managing Editor: Mary Carnis
Production Liaison: Brian Hyland
Production Editor: Janet Bolton
**Director of Manufacturing
  and Production:** Bruce Johnson
Manufacturing Manger: Ilene Sanford

Manufacturing Buyer: Cathleen Petersen
Design Director: Cheryl Asherman
Senior Design Coordinator: Miguel Ortiz
Cover Design: Robin Hoffman, Brand X Studios
Cover Art: Sarah Leen, Getty Images/National
  Geographic
Printing and Binding: R.R. Donnelley, Harrisinburg
Proofreader: Maine Proofreading Services
Copy Editor: Maine Proofreading Services

Pearson Education LTD.
Pearson Education Australia PTY, Limited
Pearson Education Singapore, Pte. Ltd.
Pearson Education North Asia Ltd.
Pearson Education Canada, Ltd.
Pearson Educacion de Mexico, S.A. de C.V.
Pearson Education—Japan
Pearson Education Malaysia, Pte. Ltd.
Pearson Education, Upper Saddle River, New Jersey

10 9 8 7 6 5 4 3 2 1
ISBN 0-13-112371-8

This is dedicated to my father, Gary Copes, who has been in law enforcement a very long time and has experienced the many sources and consequences of police stress.

Contents

❖

Preface

If asked whether they believe policing to be more stressful than other occupations, most people, relying on their stereotypical understanding of policing, would answer yes. But does research on policing support this conclusion? Interestingly, researchers offer various answers to this question, and there is nowhere near unanimous agreement that policing is as stressful as people suppose. Some argue that in addition to the routine stressors of employment, police must confront dangerous and traumatic situations (e.g., high-speed pursuits, killing someone in the line of duty, and being physically attacked) that individuals in other occupations never face. Others contend that these high-stress situations occur so infrequently that the typical officer will never experience them and therefore they cannot be a significant source of stress. They contend that policing is really no more stressful than any other occupation.

While there is no consensus regarding whether policing is more stressful than other occupations, most agree that job-related stress is an important issue for police. In fact, nearly every text on policing covers stress in detail; some even devote an entire chapter to it. One reason most authors of policing texts include a section on stress is because of the potential consequences of too much stress on officers. The effects of prolonged exposure to stressors are clear and include numerous physical, psychological, and social ailments. Physically, police officers are thought to experience high rates of disorders such as coronary heart disease, sleeping disorders, migraine headaches, and stomach ulcers. In terms of emotional problems, some studies show that police officers have high rates of anxiety and posttraumatic stress disorder. Stress-related factors have been linked to the high rates of suicide, divorce, and substance abuse among officers. Additional consequences of chronic stress in the profession include a high incidence of low job satisfaction, absenteeism, burnout, and premature retirement. It is clear that stressed employees perform poorly on their job. This is especially pertinent for police officers, as one of the primary goals of policing is to serve the public, and when officers fail to meet this goal, the community may unduly suffer. In short, some scholars argue that members of the policing profession face numerous stressors that they are improperly coping with, and as a result, their professional and personal lives are disrupted.

It may say something about employment in our society that we must continue to debate whether policing, which has never been highly coveted or materially rewarding, is a stressful occupation. Nevertheless, considering the potential adverse consequences on the well-being of officers and the community, it may be particularly important for those pursuing a career in policing to understand the sources of stress, its potential consequences, and the most effective ways to cope with it. After all, general job performance, decisions, and demeanor by police have serious consequences. This volume addresses the topic of police stress by bringing together top scholars from across the globe, including those from the United States, Canada, New Zealand, and Australia. In addition, contributors to this volume come from a variety of academic fields, including sociology, psychology, criminal justice, and the health sciences, to cast the light of several disciplines on the matter.

The first section of the book, titled "Sources of Police Stress," begins with an examination of the many causes of stress for police officers. By understanding the factors and situations that bring about stress, officers may be able to avoid stressful situations or at least minimize the harm from them. This section begins with an empirical study that investigates changes in the sources of police stress after the tragedy on September 11, 2001. In this chapter, Dennis Stevens begins with an overview of the main issues regarding police stress. He discusses how to define stress, the various stages of stress, and some of the major sources of police stress as reported by previous research. Stevens then describes how the attack on 9/11 changed officers' perceptions of the major sources of police stress. To do this, he compares the results of two police stress surveys. The first one was administered before the attack on 9/11, and the second one was given after the attack. Stevens's analysis of the two surveys indicates that the consequences of the 9/11 tragedy extended well beyond that day and have caused dramatic changes in police officers' perceptions of what is and is not stressful.

Whereas Chapter 1 addresses a number of sources of stress, Chapter 2 focuses on stress arising from critical incidents. In this chapter, Douglas Paton discusses the origins of critical incident stressors that police officers must contend with. He also describes how critical incidents can be conceptualized along three phases. These phases include the alarm and mobilization phase, the response phase, and the letdown and reintegration phase. Each of these phases brings with it unique stressors of which officers need to be aware.

In Chapter 3, Judy Van Wyk discusses sources of stress that are built into the day-to-day operations of police work. Police must respond to a variety of situations, and each of these situations brings with it unique stressors. For example, police officers acknowledge that responding to domestic dispute calls is often stressful. They may arrive at a scene only to be verbally and/or physically attacked by all parties involved, or they may find a severely injured victim that they have to tend to. In addition to these overt stressors, Van Wyk argues that domestic dispute calls have a number of hidden stressors. These stressors include sexism, racism, the dynamics of partner violence, normative perceptions of family, and media and publicity. While this is not a full list of the hidden stressors associated with responding to domestic disputes, it does generate thought and discussion on the topic.

Police officers are subject to both acute and chronic stressors. Most people, including police, place greater importance on the acute stressors that police are exposed to, such as high-speed chases, forceful arrests, and being fired on by suspects. Research has shown, however, that chronic stress may actually be more damaging to officers' health. In Chapter 4, Vivian Lord describes a chronic source of stress that arises from the organization of the police department. She elaborates on the stress placed on police officers when new programs are implemented in police departments, specifically community-oriented or problem-solving policing. The ambiguity of changing roles and how the department expects officers to act is a constant source of stress. Social support systems have been found to moderate the impact of organizational stress, but these support systems need to be source-specific to work effectively.

Part II of the book focuses on what can happen if stress goes untreated. Numerous studies have shown the negative effects of police stress on police personnel. An overview of the various consequences of stress is presented in Chapter 5. Here, Kent Kerley argues that the consequences of police stress have been neglected by researchers when compared to the sources of police stress. With the exceptions of posttraumatic stress disorder and police suicide, the consequences of stress have been underresearched. His chapter is an attempt to bring readers up to date on the research on the consequences of stress. His review focuses on three broad categories of stress-related consequences, including on-the-job consequences, physical and emotional consequences, and family and relational consequences. Consequences on the job include excessive absenteeism and tardiness, burnout, corruption, and increased use of force. Physical and emotional problems associated with chronic stress include heart disease, sleep disorders, migraines, alcoholism, and an increased risk of suicide. The familial and relational problems associated with prolonged stress include domestic abuse, divorce, and reduced social interaction.

In Chapter 6, John Violanti examines the relationship between stress and disease as it applies to policing. Violanti argues that the chronic and acute stress of police work keeps the body in a state of continuous activation to guard against these stressors. This puts a great deal of wear and tear on the body. The nature of police work makes it difficult for the body to shut off the physiological responses to the stressors, thus weakening the body and making the officer more susceptible to disease and illness. This is evidenced by the fact that police officers have high rates of heart disease, cancer, diabetes, premature death, and suicide. Violanti suggests that proper interventions and programs to develop resiliency can go a long way in alleviating the health problems associated with police stress.

Suicide is the most extreme reaction to police stress. This topic is explored in Chapter 7 by author Robert Loo. Here, he presents a psychosocial model of police suicide. This model is intended to describe, explain, and predict police suicide. According to this model, suicide is the final consequence of a series of factors. The model begins by acknowledging the many stressors that police experience. But it also suggests that people experience stress differently. Personality factors such as hardiness and emotional intelligence affect how people cope with and react to stress. Those who are unable to cope effectively with stress are subject to a number of stress reactions. For those least able to cope and those who have the desire to end their lives, the ready availability of firearms makes carrying through with their plans much easier. Loo concludes his chapter with a discussion of suicide "postvention" strategies, most of which deal largely with providing help to survivors such as family, friends, and co-workers.

Police administrators have begun to recognize the serious consequences of police stress. It is common for administrators to implement or develop programs that help address the issue of police stress. In Part III of this volume, titled "Coping with Stress," the authors discuss some of the more effective strategies that have been developed by psychologists and police administrators. In Chapter 8, Nicole Leeper Piquero examines stress and coping resources used by police officers. She points out that the bulk of research on stress and its consequences is atheoretical and overemphasizes white males. To overcome this weakness in the literature, Piquero uses general strain theory to examine gender differences in police stress and coping resources in predicting violent abuse by police officers. She concludes that males experience more stress and that this stress is related to increased negative emotions. Her results suggest that officers experience and cope with stress differently. Females are subject to different stressors and coping responses than males, and thus effective coping programs must take officers' differences into account.

In Chapter 9, Christine Stephens points out that employees of many emergency-related occupations, such as policing, are at a heightened risk of developing posttraumatic stress disorder (PTSD) because of the nature of their work. Noting that there are many causes of PTSD, Stephens discusses some of the more effective preventive strategies that have been implemented, including psychological debriefing and an integrated workplace approach. She argues that psychological debriefing is an important step in preventing PTSD but that it is often not enough. A more thorough program that integrates individual factors, the social environment, and organizational factors is more effective.

In the final chapter, Robin Haarr and Merry Morash discuss the importance of emotions, gender, and race on effective coping with police stress. They point out that the bulk of research on police stress focuses on those stressors experienced by white, male officers. Consequently, programs developed to promote effective coping strategies tend to focus on those that are most effective for males. Haarr and Morash discuss some of the more common programs and models designed to help officers cope with stress, such as the transactional model. They then discuss how these programs and models could be improved upon by acknowledging that effective coping techniques vary by race and gender. They suggest that the inclusion of emotions is central to successful coping for all types of officers, including women and minorities.

This volume concludes with a summation chapter by series editor M. L. Dantzker. Here, Dantzker draws from his insights as a police officer and an academic to put the chapters into perspective. Dantzker points out that when examining police stress, we should take into account officers' ability to effectively manage and cope with it. It is clear that people interpret and cope with stress differently. In fact, some situations that are highly stressful to some officers may not be interpreted as stressful to others. This chapter reinforces the importance of studying police stress and its consequences with the hope of finding more effective coping strategies for police officers.

suicide as a maladaptive response to intolerable life situations in their personal, family, or work life that they believed they could not resolve. Here most RCMP suicides resulted from chronic stress due to the effects of more than one significant stressor, for example, the combination of marital problems and career disappointments with the resulting deterioration of self-confidence and self-worth. This theme of "suicide as escape from self" has received greater attention; Baumeister (1990) argued that this theme is capable of integrating much of the empirical evidence about suicide.

While most police suicides usually occur within the context of chronic stress, the importance of a traumatic event must be recognized as either the precipitating or triggering event to a suicide or as a major contributing factor (Violanti, 1996). For example, Loo (1986a) found that a traumatic event (e.g., a suicide in the family) was a contributing factor in five of the 35 (14 percent) RCMP suicides.

A Psychosocial Process Model of Police Suicide

This section presents a working model that proposes to describe, explain, and predict suicide among police. A grounded theory approach characterizes the development of this model because of the primary role of the existing, mainly atheoretical, empirical literature on police suicide in formulating the model. According to Glaser (1999), "grounded theory refers to a specific methodology on how to get from systematically collecting data to producing a multivariate conceptual theory. It is a total methodological package" (p. 836). Moreover, Strauss and Corbin's (1994) suggested grounded theory acknowledges that researchers are "interested in *patterns* of action and interaction between and among various types of social units (i.e., "actors") . . . [and] reciprocal changes in patterns of action/interaction and in relationships with changes of conditions either internal or external to the process itself" (p. 278). Glaser further explained, "Grounded theory tells us what is going on, tells us how to account for the participants' main concerns, and reveals access variables that allow for incremental change. Grounded theory *is what is*, not what should, could, or ought to be" (p. 840).

This model may be seen as a psychosocial model because of the central role of psychological factors, both normal and abnormal, in understanding and predicting why some police commit suicide while others do not, even though they may be subjected to similar stressful situations. Social factors are also central to the model because police officers do not work and live in isolation. Rather they are part of work units and other groups that can provide social supports for their members. The unfolding of events over time is an important dimension in understanding the causal linkages leading to suicide and predicting the likelihood of police suicide. Thus, the model is also a process model or theory. We will also see the important place that escape theory plays in this model given our earlier discussion of the police suicide literature (Baechler, 1979; Baumeister, 1990; Loo, 1986a).

Police Stressors and Moderating Variables

The model, as shown in Figure 7–1, begins with the recognition of the many sources of stressors associated with policing, as presented earlier in Table 7–1. Next, we know that different people react differently to stressors, so there is an important role for personality,

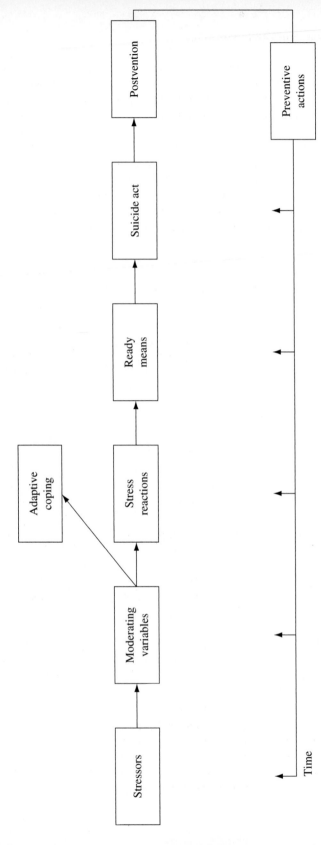

FIGURE 7–1   Model diagramming results from stressors.

Negative Affect   Agnew (1992) suggests that strain increases the likelihood that individuals will experience one or more types of negative emotions. It is these negative emotions that typically propel individuals into involvement with criminal activity. While anger is the most important of these negative emotions (Agnew, 1992), other negative emotions may also be important for understanding criminal behavior, including guilt, fear, anxiety, and depression. To examine the breadth and effect of negative emotions, three different measures of negative affect are used in this study.

The first negative affect measure is a ten-item scale representing depression. Items include (1) thoughts of ending your life, (2) headaches or pressure in head, (3) blaming self for things, (4) feeling blue, (5) nausea, upset stomach, stomach pains, (6) feeling hopeless about the future, (7) crying easily, (8) feeling tired, even with adequate sleep, (9) feeling physically and emotionally depleted, and (10) having difficulty concentrating. Items were coded from 1 (never) to 4 (always); therefore, higher values indicate more feelings of depression. These items are quite similar to those found in other depression scales in the extant literature (see Brezina, 1996; Gibson et al., 2001; Mirowsky & Ross, 1995; Piquero & Sealock, 2000).

The second measure of negative affect is anxiety. Three items indicate the respondent's level of anxiety. Respondents were asked to indicate how often they feel moody and impatient, restless, and "feel like they are at the end of the rope." Higher values indicate more anxiety.

The final measure of negative affect, cynicism, has not previously been suggested to be important by the extant theoretical and empirical GST literature but seems an appropriate negative emotion given the specific sample (i.e., police officers) used in this study. Previous policing research has established and investigated the presence of cynicism among police officers (Niederhoffer, 1967), by comparing levels of cynicism across officer rank (Regoli, Crank, & Rivera, 1990), education (Regoli, 1976), department size (Poole, Regoli, & Lotz, 1978), race (Rafky, Lawley, & Ingram, 1976), and gender (Dorsey and Giacopassi, 1986). The seven-item cynicism scale includes (1) feels no interest in things, (2) wants to withdraw from demands at work, (3) feels negative, futile, or depressed about work, (4) thinks I'm not as efficient as I should be at work, (5) interest in doing fun activities is lowered because of my work, (6) feels uncaring about the problems and needs of the public when I am at work, and (7) "when I ask myself why I get up and go to work, the only answer that occurs to me is 'I have to.' " Items were coded from 1 (never) to 4 (always) with higher values indicating greater cynicism.

Coping Skills   Agnew (1992) suggests that the utilization of coping skills helps to alleviate the effects of stress. Specifically, Agnew (1992) offers three categories of coping strategies: cognitive, emotional, and behavioral. Three measures of coping skills are utilized in this research, all of which can be classified as emotional coping strategies; that is, these are legitimate methods an individual would use to act directly on the negative emotions that result from the adversity (Agnew, 1992). The first coping skill is the purest in terms of Agnew's description of emotional coping strategies. Therefore, it is labeled emotional coping and is comprised of four items that ask the respondent the extent to which they use smoking, gambling, sexual activity, and associating with other officers at bars to deal with stressful events at work. Response options range from 1 (never) to 4 (always). The second coping skill, spiritual coping, has been used in prior GST research (Piquero & Sealock, 2000) and reflects the degree to which an individual turns to religion and prays for guidance and strength in dealing with stressful events at work. Higher values on this two-item scale indicate more use of this particular coping skill. The final coping skill, social support, is a two-item scale that indicates the degree to which the respondent turns to spouses, relatives, or friends, as well as prefers to be in the company of other people in times of stressful events. Response options range from 1 (never) to 4 (always).

Control Variables   In order to control for possible influences of education, years of experience, and race, these variables were included in the analysis. Education was coded as a dichotomous variable designed to indicate officers with no college education (coded as 0) versus those who held a college degree (coded as 1). Years of experience is a continuous variable measuring the number of years the officer has been a member of the Baltimore Police Department. This variable ranged from 0 to 44 years. Finally, the race of the officer was coded as a dichotomous variable designed to indicate white (coded as 0) officers and minority officers (coded as 1).

Dependent Variable   The outcome variable in this study is violent abuse. Respondents were asked to indicate (no/yes) whether they have ever gotten out of control and been physical (e.g., pushing, shoving, and grabbing) with (a) a fellow officer, (b) your child(ren), (c) your spouse/significant other, and (d) your pet(s). Due to the large number of no responses, this item was dichotomized as 0 (no violent abuses) and 1 (one or more violent abuses).

METHOD OF ANALYSIS

The analysis consists of both ordinary least squares (OLS) and logistic regressions estimated separately across gender. First, OLS regressions are estimated to examine the effect of strain on negative emotions. Next, logistic regression analyses are estimated for the full effects of the GST model in predicting the prevalence of domestic abuse. Each of the negative emotions is entered into its own equation because of the strong intercorrelations among the three negative emotions.

RESULTS

Table 8–1 presents descriptive statistics for all the variables as well as a series of mean-level comparisons across gender. As can be seen, six variables operated significantly across gender. For example, males were more likely to report stressors inherent to policing as well as media stress, while females reported more female-specific stressors.

Table 8–2 reports a series of OLS regressions in which each of three negative emotions is regressed on the five types of strain. These models are estimated separately across sex. As can be seen from the first column for predicting anxiety, all five strains are important predictors of anxiety among males, while only two of these stressful experiences were significantly related to anxiety among females. Specifically among females, the strain experienced from job support and the strain inherent to the police role are significantly associated with anxiety.

TABLE 8–2 Effect of Strain on Negative Emotions

Effect of Stressors	Anxiety				Depression				Cynicism			
	Males		Females		Males		Females		Males		Females	
	B	SE	B	SE	B	SE	B	SE	B	SE	B	SE
Media	-0.13*	0.06	-0.14	0.14	-0.44*	0.12	-0.09	0.37	-0.47*	0.11	-0.23	0.29
Female	0.11*	0.03	0.04	0.08	0.19*	0.06	0.25	0.20	0.23*	0.05	0.16	0.15
Police department	0.19*	0.03	0.17*	0.07	0.47*	0.06	0.57*	0.19	0.48*	0.06	0.53*	0.15
Ability	-0.14*	0.03	-0.08	0.10	-0.21*	0.07	-0.04	0.24	-0.24*	0.07	-0.16	0.19
Inherent	0.07*	0.02	0.13**	0.07	0.17*	0.05	0.43*	0.18	0.11*	0.04	0.46*	0.14
Constant	3.52*	0.48	3.68*	1.33	10.72*	1.04	7.71*	3.40	7.37*	0.95	4.85*	2.63

*$p < 0.05$; **$p < 0.10$

Turning to depression, once again all five stressors were significant predictors among male officers, while only two stressors were significantly associated with depression among females. As was the case for anxiety, the same two types of strain, job support and stress inherent to policing, were significantly associated with depression for females.

The final column of Table 8–2 reports the results for cynicism, and as can be seen they mimic those results found for both anxiety and depression among males and females. Among males, all five stressors were significantly associated with cynicism, while among females, the same two (job support and stress inherent to policing) were significantly associated with cynicism.

In sum, three important messages should be gleaned from the results in Table 8–2. First, all five stressors were associated with the experience of negative emotions among male officers, while only two stressors in particular, job support and stress inherent to policing, were significantly related to all types of negative emotions for females. Second, the female-specific stressor was unrelated to any of the negative emotions among female officers. Third, a series of coefficient comparison tests revealed that the coefficients estimated separately across gender for each of the negative emotions did not differ significantly from one another.

Table 8–3 reports a series of logistic regression estimations for the principal outcome of officer abuse (coded 0 for no abuse, 1 for at least one report of abuse). In addition to estimating the models separately across gender, each of the negative emotions is entered into its own equation because of the strong intercorrelations among the three negative emotions.

In model 1, predicting abuse, with anxiety as the key measure of negative emotions, it can be seen that only one coefficient is a significant predictor of abuse among females, namely, anxiety. Female officers who reported more anxiety also reported more abuse. This relationship between negative emotions and behavior is consistent with GST. Among male officers, three coefficients exerted a significant effect on abuse: police department stressors, emotional coping, and anxiety were significantly associated with abuse. Interestingly, and perhaps somewhat counterintuitive to GST, emotional coping was positively associated with abuse.

In model 2, with depression as the measure of negative emotions, three coefficients were significantly associated with abuse among female officers. Police department stressors, race, and depression were significant predictors of abuse. Interestingly, police department stressors were negatively related to abuse among female officers, suggesting that this source of strain runs counter to the direction anticipated by GST. Nonwhite female officers were significantly more likely to report abuse, as were female officers experiencing depression. Among the male officers, the same three variables that were important in the anxiety model are again important in the depression model. Interestingly, whereas police department stressors were negatively associated with abuse among female officers, police department stressors were positively associated with abuse among male officers. The negative emotion of depression exerted a similar, positive effect on abuse among both male and female officers.

In model 3, with cynicism as the measure of negative emotions, the same three coefficients were significant predictors of abuse among male officers: police department stressors, emotional coping, and the negative emotion of cynicism. Among female officers, only cynicism was significantly related to abuse.

TABLE 8–3 Full GST Model Predicting Violent Abuse

Variable	Model 1—Anxiety		Model 2—Depression		Model 3—Cynicism	
	Female B (SE)	Male B (SE)	Female B (SE)	Male B (SE)	Female B (SE)	Male B (SE)
Strain/Stress						
Media	0.36 (0.29)	-0.12 (0.10)	0.42 (0.32)	-0.09 (0.10)	0.43 (0.29)	-0.07 (0.10)
Personal challenges	0.03 (0.18)	0.00 (0.06)	-0.03 (0.20)	-0.00 (0.06)	0.08 (0.17)	-0.01 (0.06)
Inherent to police	-0.00 (0.14)	0.06 (0.05)	-0.07 (0.16)	0.07 (0.05)	-0.08 (0.15)	0.07 (0.05)
Police department	-0.08 (0.14)	0.13 (0.05)*	-0.29 (0.17)*	0.11 (0.05)*	-0.15 (0.14)	0.13 (0.05)*
Female	0.07 (0.15)	0.07 (0.05)	-0.08 (0.18)	0.06 (0.05)	0.06 (0.14)	0.05 (0.05)
Coping						
Emotional	-0.03 (0.19)	0.16 (0.06)*	0.01 (0.22)	0.17 (0.06)*	0.05 (0.18)	0.17 (0.06)*
Spiritual	0.17 (0.16)	-0.01 (0.06)	0.11 (0.20)	-0.04 (0.06)	0.11 (0.16)	-0.01 (0.05)
Social support	0.30 (0.23)	0.00 (0.09)	0.27 (0.26)	0.04 (0.09)	0.16 (0.22)	-0.01 (0.09)
Controls						
Education	-0.62 (0.71)	-0.25 (0.21)	-1.39 (0.90)	-0.31 (0.21)	-0.69 (0.69)	-0.33 (0.21)
Years experience	0.03 (0.05)	0.02 (0.01)	0.05 (0.06)	0.01 (0.01)	0.04 (0.05)	0.02 (0.01)
Race	0.67 (0.67)	0.13 (0.24)	1.59 (0.84)**	0.12 (0.24)	1.00 (0.65)	0.12 (0.24)
Negative Emotions						
Anxiety	0.77 (0.20)*	0.20 (0.06)*	—	—	—	—
Depression	—	—	.46 (.10)*	.13 (.03)*	—	—
Cynicism	—	—	—	—	.37 (.09)*	.10 (.03)*
Constant	-9.93 (3.58)*	-5.41 (1.20)*	-10.44 (4.01)*	-6.34 (1.25)*	-9.02 (3.41)*	-5.51 (1.22)*

*p < 0.05; **p < 0.10

135

DISCUSSION

The purpose of this study was to examine the applicability of GST as a heuristic, theoretical tool for the understanding of police officer stress, emotions, and behavior. Using data collected from the Baltimore Police Department, four main findings emerged from this effort. First, male officers report experiencing more sources of stress than female officers, and the experience of these stressors was always to increase negative emotions, regardless of how negative emotions were measured (e.g., anxiety, depression, and cynicism). Although there appeared to be differences in that some stressors were more important for male officers than female officers, a series of coefficient comparison tests failed to detect any significant differences across gender in how the different types of stressors were related to the different types of negative emotions. Second, in regression analyses predicting officer abuse, most of the stressors were insignificantly associated with abuse for both males and females, though police department stressors were positively associated with abuse among males, but negatively related to abuse among females. Third, across all regression analyses, all three negative emotions were positively related to abuse among both male and female officers. However, none of the coefficients in the regression analyses were significantly different across gender. Finally, except for emotional coping among male officers, most of the coping mechanisms were unrelated to abuse among the officers.

In sum, the results of the current study offer mixed support for GST. For example, stressful experiences were related to negative emotions in a manner consistent with GST. Similarly, three different types of negative emotions were positively related to abuse among both male and female officers. However, the coping mechanisms studied in the current effort tended to be unrelated to the type of behavior, abuse, measured in the current study. In addition, there appeared to be more similarities than differences across male and female officers in the coefficients examined in the current study, which is counter to expectations derived from Broidy and Agnew (1997).

At the same time, the data are limited in several ways which preclude any sort of definitive statement regarding the ability of GST to account for police officer strains, emotions, and behaviors. For example, only a handful of stressful experiences were examined in the current study, and all of the strains were relevant to the strain experienced within the police role. Although the data were collected with the purpose of studying police stress, future efforts should examine how stressful experiences from other domains (relationships, children, etc.) are relevant to misconduct on the job. Second, the emotional experiences measured in the current study were not necessarily situation-based. Although Agnew (1997) anticipates that there will be much overlap between situational and dispositional measures of negative emotions, this issue is far from settled (Capowich et al., 2001). Third, the data in the current study only assessed whether the officers experienced a particular stressful event. Unstudied in the current effort is the interpretation of the stressful experience. It may be that certain officers interpret certain strains in ways that may be conducive to the generation of negative emotions and criminal activity, and this may be more important for females than males (see Broidy & Agnew, 1997). Finally, only one particular outcome, abuse, was assessed in the current study. It may be that a different set of outcomes would generate different results generally, and across gender in particular.

With regard to policy, it seems that officers experience a series of negative emotions that are a function of particular police stressors. As these stressors are endemic to the police role, they also represent points of identification by the larger police department. To the extent that such stressors may be identified and minimized, then the resultant experience of negative emotions could be lessened, and consequently, the influence of negative emotions on misbehavior can be eliminated. Unfortunately, this is easier said than done, as many of the stressors examined in the current study are difficult to change. Still, it does not preclude such a focus.

In sum, the present paper has provided unique insight into the strain-emotions-behavior relationship espoused by GST as experienced by police officers in a large police department. Hopefully, future researchers will build on the preliminary analysis investigated herein and continue to develop understanding of how police officers negotiate their roles and experiences in their lines of action.

QUESTIONS FOR DISCUSSION

1. What is general strain theory and how can it be used to provide a theoretical understanding of police stress?
2. According to the current study, does the theoretical process outlined by general strain theory operate in the same way across males and females in predicting the impact of police stress on violent abuse?
3. How did the author measure strain, police stress, and the negative affects of stress? Evaluate the appropriateness of these measures.
4. Did the findings of the study provide support for the use of general strain theory as a theoretical tool for the understanding of police officer stress, emotions, and behavior?

REFERENCES

Agnew, R. (1992). Foundations for a general strain theory of crime and delinquency. *Criminology*, 30, 47–87.

Agnew, R. (1997). Stability and change in crime over the life-course: A strain theory explanation. In T. P. Thornberry (Ed.), *Developmental Theories of Crime and Delinquency: Advances in Criminological Theory* (Vol. 7) (pp. 101–132). New Brunswick, NJ: Transaction.

Agnew, R. & Brezina, T. (1997). Relational problems with peers, gender, and delinquency. *Youth and Society*, 29, 84–111.

Agnew, R. & White, H. R. (1992). An empirical test of general strain theory. *Criminology*, 30, 475–499.

Anderson, W., Swenson, D., & Clay, D. (1995). *Stress Management for Law Enforcement Officers*. Englewood Cliffs, NJ: Prentice Hall.

Anshel, M. H. (2000). A conceptual model and implications for coping with stressful events in police work. *Criminal Justice and Behavior*, 27, 375–400.

Aseltine, R. H. Jr., Gore, S., & Gordon, J. (2000). Life stress, anger and anxiety, and delinquency: An empirical test of general strain theory. *Journal of Health and Social Behavior*, 41, 256–275.

Brezina, T. (1996). Adapting to strain: An examination of delinquent coping responses. *Criminology*, 34, 39–60.

Brezina, T. (1998). Adolescent maltreatment and delinquency: The question of intervening processes. *Journal of Research in Crime and Delinquency*, 35, 71–99.

Broidy, L. (2001). A test of general strain theory. *Criminology*, 39, 9–35.

Broidy, L. & Agnew, R. (1997). Gender and crime: A general strain theory perspective. *Journal of Research in Crime and Delinquency*, 34, 275–306.

Brooks, L. W. & Piquero, N. L. (1998). Police stress: Does department size matter? *Policing: An International Journal of Police Strategies*, 21, 600–617.

Brown, J. M. & Campbell, E. A. (1994). *Stress and Policing: Sources and Strategies*. New York: John Wiley & Sons.

Capowich, G. E., Mazerolle, P., & Piquero, A. (2001). General strain theory, situational anger, and social networks: An assessment of conditioning influences. *Journal of Criminal Justice*, 29, 445–461.

Crank, J. P. & Caldero, M. (1991). The production of occupational stress in medium-sized police agencies: A survey of line officers in eight municipal departments. *Journal of Criminal Justice*, 21, 339–349.

Daly, K. & Chesney-Lind, M. (1988). Feminism and Criminology. *Justice Quarterly*, 5, 497–535.

Dorsey, R. & Giacopassi, D. (1986). Assessing gender differences in the levels of cynicism among police officers. *American Journal of Police*, 5, 91–112.

Gershon, R. (1999). *Project SHIELDS*. Washington, DC: U.S. Department of Justice, National Institute of Justice.

Gershon, R. (2000). *Police Stress and Domestic Violence in Police Families in Baltimore, Maryland,* 1997–1999 (Computer file). ICPSR version. Baltimore, MD: Johns Hopkins University (producer), 1999. Ann Arbor, MI: Inter-university Consortium for Political and Social Research (distributor).

Gibson, C. L., Swatt, M. L., & Jolicoeur, J. R. (2001). Assessing the generality of general strain theory: The relationship among occupational stress experienced by male police officers and domestic forms of violence. *Journal of Crime and Justice*, 24, 29–57.

Greenglass, E. R. (1993). The contribution of social support to coping strategies. *Applied Psychology*, 42, 323–340.

Haarr, R. N. & Morash, M. (1999). Gender, race and strategies of coping with occupational stress in policing. *Justice Quarterly*, 16, 303–336.

Hoffman, J. P. & Cerbone, F. G. (1999). Stressful life events and delinquency escalation in early adolescence. *Criminology*, 37, 343–373.

Holahan, C. J. & Moos, R. H. (1987). Personal and contextual determinants of coping strategies. *Journal of Personality and Social Psychology*, 52, 946–955.

Kroes, W. M., Margolis, B., & Hurrell, J. J. (1974). Job stress in policemen. *Journal of Police Science and Administration*, 2, 145–155.

Mazerolle, P., Burton, V. S. Jr., Cullen, F. T., Evans, T. D., & Payne, G. L. (2000). Strain, anger, and delinquent adaptations: Specifying general strain theory. *Journal of Criminal Justice*, 28, 89–102.

Mazerolle, P. & Mahs, J. (2000). General strain and delinquency: An alternative examination of conditioning influences. *Justice Quarterly*, 17, 753–777.

Mazerolle, P. & Piquero, A. (1997). Violent responses to situations of strain: A structural examination of conditioning effects. *Violence and Victims*, 12, 323–344.

Mazerolle, P. & Piquero, A. (1998). Linking exposure to strain with anger: An investigation of deviant adaptations. *Journal of Criminal Justice*, 26, 195–212.

Mirowsky, J. & Ross, C. E. (1995). Sex differences in distress: Real or artifact? *American Sociological Review*, 60, 449–468.

Morash, M. & Haarr, R. N. (1995). Gender, workplace problems, and stress in policing. *Justice Quarterly*, 12, 113–140.

Neiderhoffer, A. (1967). *Behind the Shield: The Police in Urban Society*. Garden City, NY: Doubleday.

Paternoster, R. & Mazerolle, P. (1994). General strain theory and delinquency: A replication and extension. *Journal of Research in Crime and Delinquency*, 31, 235–263.

Patterson, B. L. (1992). Job experience and perceived job stress among police, correctional, and probation/parole officers. *Criminal Justice and Behavior*, 19, 260–285.

Piquero, N. L. & Sealock, M. D. (2000). Generalizing general strain theory: An examination of an offending population. *Justice Quarterly*, 17, 449–484.

Poole, E. D., Regoli, R. M., & Lotz, R. (1978). Linkages between professionalism, work alienation, and cynicism in large and small police departments. *Social Science Quarterly*, 59, 525–534.

Rafky, D. M., Lawley, T., & Ingram, R. (1976). Are police recruits cynical? *Journal of Police Science and Administration*, 4, 352–360.

Regoli, B., Crank, J. P., & Rivera, G. F. (1990). The construction and implementation of an alternative measure of police cynicism. *Criminal Justice and Behavior*, 17, 395–409.

Regoli, R. M. (1976). An empirical assessment of Niederhoffer's police cynicism scale. *Journal of Criminal Justice*, 4, 231–241.

Spielberger, C. D., Westberry, L. G., Grier, K. S., & Greenfield, G. (1981). *Police Stress Survey: Sources of Stress in Law Enforcement*. Monograph Series 3, Number 6. Tampa, FL: University of South Florida, Human Resources Institute.

Steffensmeier, D. & Allan, E. (1996). Gender and crime: Toward a gendered theory of female offending. *Annual Review of Sociology*, 22, 459–487.

Violanti, J. M. (1985). The police stress process. *Journal of Police Science and Administration*, 13, 106–110.

Violanti, J. M. & Aron, F. (1994). Ranking police stressors. *Psychological Reports*, 75, 824–826.

Violanti, J. M. & Aron, F. (1995). Police stressors: Variations in perceptions among police personnel. *Journal of Criminal Justice*, 23, 287–294.

CASES CITED

Jacobellis v. *Ohio,* 378 U.S. 184 (1964)

9

Workplace Strategies for Prevention of PTSD

Christine Stephens

Those who work in emergency- or disaster-related occupations, such as policing, are exposed to the risk of developing psychological disorders directly related to their work. This chapter begins with an outline of the causes and incidence of posttraumatic stress disorder (PTSD) among police officers, including the kinds of events that may be traumatic and issues regarding the effects of multiple trauma, traumatic stress outside the workplace, and the health effects of traumatic stress that must be considered in an organizational context.

This is followed by a discussion of the evidence for the efficacy of preventive strategies in the work environment. First, psychological debriefing is currently considered to be one of the most common and well-known preventive strategies in use in emergency and policing organizations. Second, the elements of a broader integrated workplace approach are described in turn: individual factors, the social environment, and organizational factors. The latter two receive the most emphasis in this chapter. The social environment has received some attention lately, and the important elements that are considered here are social support, opportunities to talk about trauma at work, and attitudes regarding the expression of emotion in the workplace. Organizational factors are considered as either direct organizational support in the context of trauma or the detrimental effects of routine stressors on recovery. This area has not received sufficient investigation to date but is emerging as one of the most important aspects of recovery from work-related traumatic stress.

TRAUMATIC EXPERIENCES AND PTSD

The essential feature of PTSD is the development of a range of distressing psychological and physical symptoms following exposure to a traumatic experience (*DSM-IV*; American Psychiatric Association, 1994). Much police work involves the possibility of encountering traumatic situations, and of all the high-risk occupations, police officers may have the greatest risk of experiencing traumatic events at work (Carlier, 1999). Studies with police officers in Britain, Australia, New Zealand, and the United States have shown that the traumatic events most often reported by police include infrequently occurring duties related to violent death, injury, or the nonaccidental death of a child. They also include events that occur with more frequency, including facing violent offenders, the possibility of physical injury, and encountering an unpredictable situation (Brown & Campbell, 1990; Evans & Coman, 1993; Stephens & Miller, 1998; Violanti, 1996). Events most likely to be related to PTSD symptoms are a known police officer's death, physical assault, and chronic distress at work (Stephens & Miller, 1998).

There is evidence to demonstrate that although exposure to traumatic events is not routine for police officers, such exposures have detrimental effects for some police officers. In the United States, 12 to 35 percent of police officers suffer from PTSD, with various levels of psychological disabilities. In addition, PTSD is the fifth most frequently referred problem presented to police psychologists (Mann & Neece, 1990). Police officers can be diagnosed and treated while on the job, but many people with PTSD symptoms do not seek treatment (McFarlane, 1988). In a study of police officers in the Netherlands, Gersons (1989) found that of 37 officers who suffered PTSD symptoms, none sought any kind of treatment. These officers had complaints from their superiors about their work, but neither the superiors nor the police officers themselves understood the relationship between their inadequate role functioning and their traumatic experiences.

In addition to affects on health and job performance, untreated symptoms may lead to unacceptable levels of early retirement. In New Zealand, a study of police officers' early retirement showed that psychological factors were the predominant reason for leaving (69.2 percent) (Miller, 1996). Forty-three percent of the officers in this study reported trauma as a factor in their applications to retire, and 16.8 percent were diagnosed by health professionals as exhibiting specific symptoms of posttraumatic reactions.

Additional issues arise when investigating the symptoms of workers who encounter a wide range of potentially traumatic experiences in their lifetime. The first of these issues is the effect of cumulative traumas. It has often been assumed that experience with traumatic incidents increases the ability to withstand the effects of subsequent exposure. An opposing view is that coping abilities break down with increased exposure to pain, death, or suffering and, consequently, individuals may become psychologically debilitated (Moran & Britton, 1994). There is increasing evidence to support the latter view of a positive relationship between the number of traumatic events experienced and the severity of posttraumatic stress symptoms. Green (1994) and Violanti (1996) both cite examples of studies demonstrating that prior traumatization increases the risk of developing PTSD after events such as combat or natural disasters. In a large community sample, Vrana and Lauterbach (1994) found that the highest rates of PTSD were among those who had suffered multiple traumas.

Williams (1993) offers a theoretical explanation of the effects of additional traumatic experiences. If individuals have not successfully resolved previous trauma, they may "stair-step" to more pathological reactions to the new event, and workers who are particularly at risk for these stair-stepping effects of stress exposure include police officers. Moran and Britton (1994) conducted a study that supports Williams's theory. A survey of 210 volunteer emergency workers demonstrated no association between a number of personality variables and the severity or length of reaction to a traumatic experience. However, the greater number of incidents attended and more years of service were predictive of the duration and the severity of the stress reaction. Similarly, Stephens and Miller (1998) found that among 526 police officers who had varying lengths of service, the number of different traumatic events experienced on the job was correlated with the strength of PTSD symptoms. Additionally, repeated experience of the same type of event predicted higher PTSD scores. This observation was replicated among 263 police officers who had only six months' work experience. While taking into account the officers' PTSD scores at entry to police college and their other life experiences, Huddleston (2002) found that the number of events experienced in only six months on the job was already significantly correlated with PTSD symptoms. Such observations indicate that repeated exposure to traumatic events is not likely to inoculate young officers against the distressing or horrifying aspects of police work but rather increase their risks of psychological disorder following traumatic event exposure in the course of their police careers.

A second issue related to police trauma is whether the traumatic stressors that affect workers' health are associated more with their job than with other life experiences. It has already been demonstrated that there is a percentage of people suffering from trauma and PTSD symptoms in the general civilian population (Norris, 1992; Vrana & Lauterbach, 1994). Two studies carried out in New Zealand showed that police recruits might enter training with very high rates of trauma experiences (Huddleston, 2002; Stephens, Long, & Flett, 1999). In these two samples of recruits, 32.6 percent and 40.7 percent had experienced an assault (compared to 15 percent identified by Norris [1992] using the same schedule), and 23.5 percent and 15.1 percent of female recruits reported sexual assault (7.3 percent in Norris's sample). Although it has also been shown (Huddleston, 2002; Stephens & Miller, 1998) that PTSD symptoms among police officers are generally related to trauma experienced after joining the police, and trauma experienced on duty as a police officer is more strongly related to PTSD symptoms than trauma experienced while off duty, high rates of traumatic stress in earlier life suggest that police officers may begin work predisposed to the cumulative effects of traumatic stress. Such preliminary evidence lends weight to Paton's (1997) call for norms to be established for different occupational groups on which to base further research into the effects of occupational trauma.

A third important issue is the close relationship of PTSD with physical health. A diagnosis of PTSD includes some physical symptoms, such as insomnia; however, there are many other harmful physiological effects of stress that have been documented in experimental and epidemiological studies (see Solomon, Mikulincer, & Habershaim, 1990). PTSD has been reliably linked with several other illnesses and disabilities, such as alcoholism and drug dependence, somatization disorder, anxiety disorders, and major depression, which are often manifested and measured in terms of somatic symptoms (Sutker, Uddo-Crane, & Allain, 1991). Many investigators have found PTSD symptoms strongly associated with reports of poor physical health and physiological complaints in war veterans from the United States, Israel, and New Zealand. In a sample of 527 New Zealand police officers surveyed by questionnaire, there was a strong correlation between PTSD and physical health (Stephens & Miller, 1998). Those officers whose symptoms were severe enough to be classified as PTSD cases (12 percent) reported significantly more physical symptoms, poorer self-reported health, and more disability days than the others. A study of the effects of police shootings found that the three officers with a severe case of PTSD identified in interviews also suffered from other symptoms such as severe depression, digestive upsets, migraine headaches, and loss of sensation in the right side of the body (Manolias & Hyatt-Williams, 1993).

It is apparent that along with the disabling symptoms of PTSD, people who develop the disorder following traumatic experiences are likely to suffer from a range of other incapacitating physical symptoms that may affect their working lives. There is a direct impact on police work from physical impairment, as police officers must maintain a certain level of fitness to carry out their duties. It is in the testing of police officers for physical health symptoms that the effects of stress may be noticed. It has been noted that the physical symptoms of stress may be apparent before a psychiatric diagnosis is made and that these symptoms are not usually linked to a medically diagnosed disorder. McFarlane, Atchison, Rafalowicz, and Papay (1994) reported that general practitioners did not relate physical symptoms in PTSD sufferers with their psychiatric disorder, although general practitioners who treat police officers are likely to be the first to be presented with the physical symptoms of traumatic stress.

It is important to realize that the prevalence of PTSD symptoms among working police officers is often similar to that in other civilian populations that have experienced a traumatic event (Huddleston, 2002; Stephens & Miller, 1998). As in these populations, most individuals do recover from trauma and do not develop disorders. However, it is also noteworthy that an increased number of work-related traumatic experiences are associated with higher PTSD symptoms and the particular traumatic experiences that are related to PTSD are more likely to be part of police work. Any notable increases in PTSD symptoms are reliably associated with other health deficits, therefore police officers who suffer from traumatic stress will have poorer psychological and physical health. Those officers who may be categorized as suffering from PTSD (7 to 13 percent, according to Stephens and Miller, 1998) will require extensive additional care and are at risk of early retirement. Taken together, this means that police organizations must take responsibility for the effects of work-related stress and, given that exposure to traumatic stress is often an unavoidable aspect of the job, pay serious attention to strategies that prevent the development of symptoms in officers who are susceptible to traumatic experiences.

PREVENTIVE STRATEGIES

Psychological Debriefing

Organizations whose workers risk traumatic exposure are increasingly interested in preventing sequelae, such as posttraumatic stress disorder (PTSD), and a variety of other damaging effects on health. A common intervention is the provision of psychological debriefing for organized groups following exposure to trauma. There are several debriefing protocols, but the basic elements are common to most forms, and the sources and details of these debriefing protocols are described by Shalev (1994). Bisson and Deahl (1994) also describe the history and purpose of the intervention and its structure as a single group meeting, two to three days after the event, which lasts approximately two hours. Although psychological debriefing has theoretical rationale and strong support from many practitioners, much of this support is anecdotal and there is a need for further empirical study to examine the immediate and long-term effects of such interventions. The results of the evaluation of debriefing to date are mixed but provide reason to be cautious about the routine provision of debriefing without additional support in organizational settings.

Bisson and Deahl (1994) cite examples of studies that support the effectiveness of early psychological intervention that have been flawed for at least one of several reasons: they assessed only the subjective, immediate reactions of participants and no long-term outcomes; there were no control groups; or their results were thrown into doubt by other contradictory findings. Other studies have employed comparison groups of people who have experienced the same event and have not attended a debriefing. These studies have not found any differences in psychological stress symptoms for those who were debriefed at two weeks (Hytten & Hasle, 1989), six months (Brom, Kleber, & Hofman, 1993), nine months (Deahl, Gillham, Thomas, Searle, & Srinivasan, 1994), or up to two years (Kenardy, Webster, Lewin, Carr, Hazell, & Carter, 1996) after the traumatic event. Some studies have even attributed detrimental effects to debriefing. For example, Griffiths & Watts (1992) found that emergency workers who had been debriefed following bus crashes had significantly higher symptom scores one year later than those who were not debriefed. These early contradictory findings have led to more recent attempts to conduct systematic reviews of debriefing evaluations. A review conducted by Wessely, Rose, and Bisson (1999) included only studies that employed randomized controlled trials, standardized and valid measures, and the provision of a structured intervention within one month of the traumatic event. Only six studies fulfilled these criteria, and Wessely et al. concluded that debriefing did not appear to reduce psychological distress in the short term nor was it found to be successful in preventing PTSD. At the same time, Everly, Boyle, and Lating (1999) conducted a meta-analysis of the evaluation literature using ten adequately controlled studies from peer-reviewed journal articles and clinical proceedings as the database. The results of this meta-analysis supported the effectiveness of group psychological debriefings in alleviating the effects of vicarious psychological distress in emergency care providers. Accordingly, the effectiveness of debriefing to reduce psychological sequelae is still uncertain, and although debriefing may provide some short-term benefits, the long-term benefits are unknown.

Among the difficulties that have been encountered in attempting to evaluate debriefing programs in organizational contexts are that the aims and procedures of debriefing practices have not been standardized and the processes of providing debriefings do not always function well. Management practices are an important aspect of the provision of such support services, and these may be inadequate in regard to ensuring that affected officers have access to debriefing when it is appropriate. Also, the provision of mandatory debriefings may be met with resistance by staff for various reasons (Stephens, 1997). Taken together, these difficulties and the uncertain effects of debriefing suggest that other aspects of the organizational environment must be taken into account when considering the prevention of PTSD or other health effects of trauma. The provision of a one-off debriefing session alone is not the solution to organizational responsibility for the recovery of officers from traumatic experiences.

Elements of Integrated Responses to Traumatic Stress

Harvey (1996) has proposed a multidimensional definition of trauma recovery. Harvey argues that the efficacy of an intervention depends on its fit with the recovery environment and, accordingly, provides an ecological model of trauma recovery that includes person, event, and environmental factors. Stephens (1997) demonstrated the importance of a number of aspects of the posttrauma environment: social support, workplace attitudes, and education are related to PTSD symptoms. Such findings support suggestions (Raphael, Meldrum, & McFarlane, 1995) that whatever the contribution of psychological debriefing to the reduction of posttraumatic stress symptoms, there are other variables in the environment that also contribute to recovery and must be considered by responsible organizations and health professionals. The following sections address these other aspects, including the individual person factors, the social factors, and the organizational factors that contribute to recovery.

Person Characteristics   Thompson and Solomon (1991) found that a police body recovery team had lower psychological symptom scores compared to other similar teams. In addition to debriefing sessions and ongoing management support, they attributed this result to the careful selection and training of the individuals involved. This comment points to two discrete paths for the possible implementation of understandings how individual differences are related to vulnerability to traumatic stress reactions.

In regard to selection, Thompson and Solomon (1991) suggested that their findings pointed to the importance of the selection of stable extroverted individuals. Other authors (Deahl et al., 1994) have also suggested that selection for particular personal characteristics would be useful, although which particular characteristics are helpful is not yet established. The important person variables that may contribute to traumatic stress suggested by Harvey (1996) were the initial distress level, intelligence, and personality. Bartone (2000) has pointed to hardiness as an important personality characteristic in this context. Raphael et al. (1995) included personal coping resources, as well as cognitive impairments, past psychological morbidity, and other life stresses. Stephens and Miller (1998) found that officers with no educational qualifications were likely to have higher PTSD scores, which is consistent with previous findings in other populations (e.g., Norris, 1992). Together, these findings point to a group of characteristics to be measured and screened for. However, more research is required to clarify the characteristics of vulnerable individuals and the ways in which this knowledge may be used ethically to screen individuals for particular types of work or for particular types of attention following trauma.

The second strategy to address individual characteristics was training. Thompson and Solomon (1991) argued that careful training in carrying out their task contributed to the psychological health of police officers involved in body recovery work. This strategy is particularly applicable to the preparation of groups of officers who are assigned in advance to potentially disturbing tasks such as body recovery or disaster work. Alexander and Wells (1991) also studied the reactions of police body recovery teams after a major disaster. They tested 48 police officers who were involved in body-handling duties following the explosion of the Piper Alpha oil rig and 42 controls. Once again, the officers involved in disaster duties did not show high levels of posttraumatic distress or psychiatric morbidity, and these results were interpreted in terms of the officers' individual coping strategies (as well as organizational and managerial factors). It would be beneficial to include the development of such coping skills in officer training. Recently there has been increasing emphasis placed on the importance of modeling positive responses to change and unpredictability to foster characteristics such as resiliency (Bartone, 2000) and on training for cognitive models that allow adaptive responses to emergency, which will lead to positive resolution of distressing experiences. These models of training will allow officers to be prepared to cope with unexpected traumatic events or the cognitive reactions to distressing tasks.

Social Environment   Greenberg (1995) and Harvey (1996) have summarized calls for attention to the mechanisms that result in successful adaptation to trauma, and both suggest a focus on the study of resilience and recovery rather than the focus on negative pathological reactions. This call has been echoed in occupational areas of study. For example, Dunning (1999) proposes a turn to emphasize the healthy and adaptive ways of coping with stressful events within organizations. An emphasis on social support as an integral aspect of the long-term recovery environment will be an important aspect of this shift in emphasis. Social support has received increasing attention as an important variable that intervenes between the traumatic experience and PTSD. The initial evidence for the importance of social support in preventing adverse long-term psychological disorders, especially PTSD, came chiefly from work with combat veterans and the victims of natural disasters (see Stephens & Long, 1999). Most evidence demonstrates significant positive effects for social support: the more social support resources that individuals report, the fewer their PTSD symptoms. For example, Boscarino (1995) found that lower social support was associated with higher PTSD symptoms, anxiety, depression, and alcohol abuse in 2,490 Vietnam veterans, and he suggested that the role of social support should not be overlooked in the study of those subjected to traumatic stressors.

Social support for working police officers may be provided by a variety of sources such as work supervisors or nonwork sources such as family and friends. Studies have demonstrated the importance of both co-worker and supervisor support as a moderator of the effects of stress. Kaufmann and Beehr (1989) suggest that among police officers, support from both supervisors and co-workers is more important, in regard to relieving the effects of work-related stressors, than support from people external to the organization. Stephens & Long (1999) focused on the role of social support in moderating the effects of traumatic stress in their study of 527 New Zealand police officers. Their results suggest that police officers who have more traumatic experiences are less likely to have symptoms of psychological disorder if they also receive more support from their colleagues at work. In this same study, higher support from the officers' peers, supervisors, and from nonwork sources were all directly related to lower PTSD symptoms, regardless of the level of trauma. There may well be different functional pathways for different sources of support. For example, peer support offers the best opportunities for the discussion of traumatic experiences, which is helpful in the recovery from trauma; supervisors may have the opportunity to be supportive by preventing organizational stressors; and family members may provide other emotional support.

In addition to the sources of support, the type of support that is provided deserves closer attention. The effects of social support have been found to vary according to the types of stress that police officers experience. Cohen and Wills (1985) have proposed that social support moderates the effects of stress when the social support functions enhance coping abilities specifically related to needs elicited by the stressful event. Hence, it would be useful to isolate the coping functions of social support that are specifically related to the needs elicited by the experience of trauma. Theoretical understandings and empirical observations suggest that the coping ability that would be supportive in the case of trauma is the need to talk about the experience and to express emotions connected with it. When Stephens, Long, & Miller (1997) included emotional support and talk about trauma as aspects of social support, the variance in PTSD scores that was explained by these social support measures was higher than that explained by the number of traumatic experiences. The following sections will examine these specific aspects of social support in more detail.

In the wider social support area, Barnes and Duck (1994) have proposed that it is daily talk that provides the transactional background for social support in crisis situations. Fenlason and Beehr (1994) also describe communication as part of the conceptual definition of social support and provide evidence showing that everyday communications are an important part of the provision of emotional social support. In the context of traumatic experiences, Bootzin (1997) suggests that the observed benefits to health of both social support and communication are part of the same relationship because social interaction provides opportunities for people to talk about and integrate emotional experiences.

Horowitz (1993) presents an information-processing conceptualization of PTSD in which emotional processing of the trauma is necessary for the PTSD symptoms to decline. According to Horowitz, the process of working through includes talking about the trauma and its related emotions so that the experience can be assimilated. The persistence of symptoms in chronic PTSD sufferers could be due to factors that hinder emotional processing, including avoidance. A common manifestation of avoidance is refraining from talking about the trauma, so a socially supportive environment should enhance recovery from trauma through encouragement of discussion of the event. Studies of Vietnam veterans in the United States have suggested that veterans need to talk openly about and fully explore their combat experiences in a nonjudgmental atmosphere to recover from trauma and that chronic PTSD sufferers had been unable to assimilate their combat experiences in this way. Norman (1988) interviewed nurses who had served in Vietnam and found that apart from the intensity of the stressor, the other variable correlated with PTSD was the strength of the social network. Typically, those nurses who did not suffer from PTSD were more likely to have been in touch with people who had shared the experience and with whom they could discuss their experiences. These examples support the view of Williams (1993), who holds that in occupational contexts, such as police, it is helpful to express feelings connected with the trauma and this sort of talk about trauma is particularly effective when shared with those who have experienced similar events, such as peers at work.

An important aspect of talking about traumatic experiences is the content of communication between people who are giving and receiving support; this is also related to the suggestions that talking about aspects of traumatic experience is the important component of support. Among the police officers who participated in the Stephens et al. (1997) study, social support measured as emotional support and talking about trauma was associated with decreased PTSD symptoms. However, communication about negative aspects of work, with either peers or supervisors, was associated with *increased* PTSD symptoms. These results suggest that if social support is seen in terms of interactions with others, then only some types of communication are supportive; other types are related to poor health outcomes. Solomon et al. (1990) discuss the evidence for a distinction between social support and social interaction in which negative interactions are seen not as part of a support continuum but as stressors. There are many aspects of social interactions that may be burdensome, and it is important to identify the specific types of social support that are beneficial.

Stephens and Long (2000) examined social support as a moderator of traumatic stress in terms of these specific support needs. Their findings showed that levels of particular types of communication were directly related to PTSD and physical symptoms (after taking the effects of traumatic experiences into account). These types included communications about disturbing events and about positive aspects of the workplace with peers and communications about nonwork matters or negative aspects of the workplace with the supervisor.

Positive and negative communications about work and communications about disturbing experiences with peers (not supervisors) were shown to moderate the relationship between trauma and PTSD or physical symptoms. High levels of positive talk about work were related to a significantly weakened trauma-physical symptoms relationship, and this beneficial effect of social interaction was expected. Barnes and Duck (1994) suggest that everyday communicative contexts make the provision of crisis-related interactions possible. Thus, the nature of casual socializing will provide the background for more directly supportive communication. It is possible that more positively framed, work-related talk provides a positive (and apparently beneficial) background for the assimilation of work-related experiences, including trauma.

The second important result was in regard to talk about trauma itself, as well as negative work communications. Moderate levels of talk (and not low or high levels) about disturbing experiences and moderate levels of negative talk about work (such as complaints about the workplace) were both associated with a weaker trauma-strain relationship. Thus, talk about disturbing experiences and negative talk about work may be helpful but apparently have no supportive effect when they are either too low or too high. These findings support the suggestions of Bootzin (1997) that talk about distressing experiences will ameliorate the health effects of trauma by contributing to the cognitive processing of that experience, but only up to a point. Moderate levels of talk may be beneficial, but at high levels of such talk, the trauma-strain relationship is again stronger. Negative talk about work seems to be functioning in a similar way, which suggests that complaining about work conditions is detrimental if there is too much of this sort of talk.

Communications about nonwork matters with peers also interacted with traumatic experiences, in that their association with PTSD or physical symptoms was *stronger* if there were more communications. At low levels of talk about nonwork matters, the trauma-strain relationship was weak and nonsignificant, whereas at moderate and high levels, it was stronger and significantly correlated. High levels of communication with peers regarding nonwork matters may not be helpful in the case of trauma, due to an escapist or distracting function of nonwork talk that has been suggested by Fenlason and Beehr (1994) and that would not allow for the processing of traumatic experiences. This is also accounted for by Horowitz's (1993) theory of PTSD, in which denial and avoidance of the experience contribute toward the development of the disorder.

Negative communication with a supervisor about work were also found to weaken the trauma-strain relationship at both high and low levels of communication. This result points to the need to consider not only the important differences between supervisors and peers as sources of different types of communication but also what the levels communication might be. For instance, as stressful experiences increase negative perceptions of work, police officers may find relief in complaining about work. However, too much complaining about work or talk with peers about disturbing experiences may become burdensome, although apparently not if such talk is with the supervisor.

Together, these results point to the differential impact of different types of communication with peers. Considering communication in the workplace as a specific function of social support is useful, but it is also important to attend to the different aspects of communication itself. The Stephens and Long (2000) study highlighted some interesting relationships among these communication variables about traumatic experiences and health outcomes. A further important difference highlighted by the analysis was that most of the supervisor communication variables did not buffer the trauma-strain relationship, showing that the source of support is also important. Fenlason and Beehr (1994) also found that communications with the supervisor were not necessarily the most important in buffering work-related stressors. In the case of traumatic stress, communication with peers have more impact on the stress-strain relationship. As Barnes and Duck (1994) point out, in crisis situations people initially turn to those with whom they have continuous relationships. This everyday continuity may be generally better established with peers than with supervisors.

The demonstrated importance of communications with peers and the provision of a balance between the beneficial effects of talk about distressing experiences and the harmful effects that communications may have supports the development of a positive, supportive work environment for officers and interventions such as peer support programs (Paton, 1997). Such programs include the provision of trained individuals who are able to meet the need for communication without breaking down workplace mores of nondisclosure that work to protect the larger group from the damaging effects of too much disclosure.

Following from recognition of the importance of communications in the social environment is concern about how easy it is for police officers to talk about their traumatic experiences and the emotions connected with them in the workplace. If the opportunities to discuss traumatic events and express associated emotions are shown to help prevent the development of PTSD and other health problems, then this type of emotional support among the members of an organization such as the police would be salutary. The ease of talking about trauma must be taken into account, as it is well documented that there are some workplaces in which it is not socially acceptable to disclose distress, and it has been recognized that members of police organizations often have negative attitudes toward the expression of emotions. Indications of the quality of police communications within work groups come from research that has been carried out on police personality and attitudes. Police culture in Britain, the Netherlands, the United States, and Australia has been found to include stances that involve the denial of emotions (Mann & Neece, 1990; Pogrebin & Poole, 1991). There is a general tendency for officers to show little caring or respect for others' feelings (Evans, Coman, & Stanley, 1992), and the sharing of emotional experiences is an aspect of support that is not always found in police culture. These studies show that police officers may disguise emotions for fear of revealing personal flaws or not measuring up to an ethic of macho toughness.

Thus, the prevailing attitudes observed in many studies of police work culture do not permit the self-disclosure that allows therapeutic support, and police attitudes may be hindering the therapeutic responses necessary for recovery from adverse reactions to trauma. In this way, social support at work could even be encouraging the development of PTSD in some individuals. It is important to note here that police traits are developed by the work situation and therefore vary between cultures and between police forces in the same society. There is evidence from a range of countries that suggests that some generalizations may be made about the nature of police work, but the potential for wide variations must be also taken into account. It seems likely that individuals in police groups who do have a strong "toughness" ethic, in which the expression and even the experience of emotion are denied, are likely to be more at risk for developing PTSD following traumatic experiences.

Stephens, Long, and Miller (1997) examined the relationship between attitudes to expressing emotions at work and PTSD symptoms. They demonstrated that police officers who feel able to express their emotions and allow others to do the same are less likely to develop PTSD symptoms. When controlling for the effects of all other social support variables on PTSD scores, it was found that attitudes to expressing emotion about trauma significantly moderated the impact of trauma on PTSD symptoms. When officers reported positive attitudes toward the expression of emotion in their workplace, the relationship between their traumatic experiences and PTSD symptoms was significantly weakened. The police officers who had traumatic experiences were less likely to show symptoms of psychological disorder if they perceived that people were able to express emotions at their workplace.

Stephens and Long (2000) also found that the ease of talking about trauma at work was one of the most important aspects of communication in direct relation to PTSD symptoms and to the reported number of physical symptoms. The perception of the ease of talking about traumatic experiences at work moderated the relationship between PTSD and physical symptoms in police officers in that the easier it was for officers to talk about trauma at work, the less likely their traumatic experiences were to be associated with PTSD or physical symptoms. In addition, the ease of talking about trauma was found to compensate somewhat for the negative impact of talk about disturbing experiences on PTSD symptoms. If officers perceived that it was easy to talk about such matters in their workplace, the positive effects of this on PTSD symptoms tended to ameliorate the negative effects of other workplace attributes. Thus, a perception that it is very easy to talk about traumatic experiences at work may be considered particularly beneficial for the health of those officers with higher levels of traumatic experience.

Social support has been examined as one of the important variables that may influence recovery following the experience of trauma. Emotional support from others, which provides opportunities to express emotions, is one environmental influence that can facilitate cognitive adaptation efforts. Such support includes understanding of the types and sources of workplace communications that may be supportive or detrimental and the importance of a workplace culture that allows for the appropriate levels of talk about traumatic events and the expression of emotion associated with traumatic experiences. The investigation of the effects of emotional social support and the provision of such support, and a closer study of attitudes regarding the expression of emotion in the workplace, will improve our understanding of the contribution of these aspects of support to the cognitive processing of traumatic memories. The results of studies of the environment in which recovery takes place are also directly applicable to the development of workplace interventions that recognize existing coping skills and emphasize positive coping following traumatic stress.

Organizational Factors   The negative effects of high levels of negative communications about work on the stressor-strain relationship, reported by Stephens and Long (2000), also suggest that police officers suffer if they have too much to complain about in the workplace, but it is beneficial if such complaints can be made to their supervisors. This draws our attention to the detrimental or positive effects of organizational factors in the trauma recovery environment. Organizational factors, although previously recognized as a major source of stress to police officers, have received little research attention in the area of occupational traumatic stress. This final section will touch on the need to consider the organizational environment in two broad ways: as a source of support for police officers who have experienced traumatic stress and as a moderator of the effects of trauma on the development of disorder.

In the studies of body recovery teams whose members had positive outcomes following potentially traumatic experiences, the authors suggested that organizational support was a very important aspect of successful recovery. Thompson and Solomon (1991) found that a police body recovery team had lower symptom scores compared to other similar teams, and they attributed this to ongoing managerial support, as well as critical incident debriefing sessions that were managed as part of the group routine. Alexander (1993) reported that the majority of 35 police officers, three years following their involvement in the retrieval and identification of human remains after a major disaster, were also free from signs of psychiatric morbidity. The officers involved in this study reported the following features of their particular work situation that were helpful: high morale, a clear definition of duties, helpful feedback about their work, good relationships among all staff (including between junior and senior officers), being given a feeling that they were engaged in a valuable task, and having attention paid to their physical and emotional needs. This does not mean that the officers were not distressed by the body retrieval task but rather that distress was not related to later psychological problems. Alexander suggested that in this situation organizational and managerial practices appeared to be powerful antidotes to adverse posttraumatic reactions. These suggestions emphasize the importance of developing managerial capability to facilitate trauma interventions. They suggest that it would be helpful if managers of workers who are at risk for traumatic stress were trained to develop a supportive and participative management style that can assist with the identification, acknowledgment, and acceptance of staff needs and with managing recovery.

Apart from managerial focus on the needs of those who have been involved in traumatic experiences, recent research has shown that the more general organizational factors, such as workload or unfair work practices, have an important impact on psychological outcomes for police officers and may also interact with traumatic experiences to increase the possibilities of developing psychological or physical disorders that are related to PTSD (Sloan, Rozensky, Kaplan, & Saunders, 1994; Stephens, 1996).

There is a growing body of evidence suggesting that organizational stressors are more psychologically damaging than traumatic stressors. Brown and Campbell (1990) investigated the perceived effects of police organizational and operational stressors in a sample of 954 police officers from an English provincial police force. The definition of operational stressors was broadly based and included such experiences as dealing with sudden deaths, violent offenders, and the victims of violence. These events emerged as the most frequently reported operational stressors. The organizational or management stressors that were the most frequently reported sources of felt stress for more than half of the sample were staff and manpower shortages, shift work, time pressures and deadlines, lack of consultation, and communication difficulties. When the police officers were interviewed about these stressors, they identified organizational and management factors four times more often than operational duties as the most stressful.

To compare the effects of these different sources of stress on psychological symptoms, Evans and Coman (1993) surveyed 271 police officers from Australian police organizations and examined work stressors under two categories: job content stressors (those that arose from the duties that police officers carried out) and job context stressors (those that arose from the work situation and the nature of the police organization in which the officers performed their duties). Job context stressors related to perceived difficulties in the job environment and included such things as unsafe working conditions, lack of effective communication, inadequate career opportunities, narrow latitude with respect to decision making, and role ambiguity. The results from this study indicated that although Australian police officers were occasionally involved in highly stressful job content events (e.g., the violent death of a partner in the line of duty, shooting someone in the line of duty, or attending a call to the nonaccidental death of a child), these events were perceived to be a necessary aspect of the job. In contrast, the officers were frequently exposed to moderately stressful job context events that derived from the nature of the organization in which they worked. The most frequently occurring job context events were long hours, job overload, change in supervisors, negative community attitudes, changing shifts, and duty under a poor supervisor. The officers also described their police organizations as poorly equipped to maintain their own organizational systems and lacking the flexibility to adapt to new environmental and social circumstances. The police officers felt there was little chance of personal growth and development and that instead they were bound to operate within narrow and inflexible rules and guidelines.

Evans and Coman (1993) accordingly suggested that the major source of stress for police officers came from the organization in which they worked, and this has continued to be supported. For example, Violanti and Aron (1995) studied 110 police officers from a large police department in New York State and found that organizational stressors affected psychological distress more than six times as much as operational police stressors such as body handling or violent offenses. Hart, Wearing, and Headey (1995) examined the organizational stressors in police work in more detail and included positive as well as negative aspects of organizational practice. The work experiences of police officers were framed in terms of two broad domains of experience that related to daily organizational and operational experiences: organizational hassles (organizational stressors as daily negative events) and uplifts (daily positive events); both were defined as those experiences stemming from the day-to-day routines of police organizations. The uplifts that were found to be important were daily issues related to supervision, amenities, administration, co-workers, workload, and decision making. A survey of Australian police officers based on this conceptualization of sources of stress found that as in other studies of police stress, organizational rather than operational experiences were more important in relation to psychological well-being. Furthermore, positive and negative work experiences were shown to contribute independently to an officer's well-being. Both positive and negative aspects of the work environment must be considered, as the existence of one does not offset the effects of the other.

Huddleston (2002) tested these measures in a prospective study of 314 police officers in New Zealand. Baseline measures were taken when the officers were first recruited and as they started their training, and second wave measures were made after they had worked for six months as police officers. Although these officers had a short time on the job, the effects of varying levels of positive or negative aspects of the workplace were evident. Organizational stressors were associated with psychological distress and were more strongly related to psychological distress than traumatic events. Organizational uplifts were not related to psychological distress, but these daily positive events were associated with better physical health.

Thus, it is necessary to appreciate the importance of the organizational environment and the effects on psychological and physical health that must be taken into account. Although these effects have a stronger effect on health in general than the traumatic aspects of police work, this does not mean that the damaging effects of traumatic stress should be ignored because they affect a small number of officers. In regard to trauma, the most interesting question that follows these understandings about the importance of the organizational environment is, how do these practices affect the ongoing recovery of the individual who has been traumatized?

When analyzing the data from the New Zealand police trauma study described above (Stephens, 1996), it was found that talking about distressing experiences was not beneficial for officers if they were also complaining about their workplace. If the officers were more likely to talk about negative aspects of the workplace, any beneficial effects of discussing disturbing experiences, in terms of lower PTSD symptoms, were more likely to be lost. These results highlighted the many complaints that the researchers had already received about work conditions; although the research was focused on issues related to traumatic stress, the participants did not wish to ignore the other sources of stress at work. This observation supported the previous work that has called attention to the importance of routine stressors in police work.

When other investigators of traumatic stress have taken organizational aspects into account, similar findings are reported. Sloan et al., (1994) described the effects of a shooting incident in an elementary school in terms of the stress experienced by public safety, mental health, and medical personnel. Their results showed that a self-reported heavy workload and time pressure at work were related to PTSD symptoms both immediately after and at the six-month anniversary of the incident. A recent study of 700 U.S. police officers with 350 matched controls (Best, Brunet, Weiss, Metzler, Rogers, Rosario, Fagan, & Marmar, 2000) also found that routine work stress was the most important factor regarding the development of posttraumatic stress reactions. The most troublesome work stressors reported in this study were being underpaid, work demands, public criticism, and unfair criminal sentencing. Paton, Smith, Ramsay, and Akande (1999) examined organizational influences on traumatic reactivity across different occupational groups and showed that the organizational environment influenced traumatic stress reactions in high-risk professions.

Huddleston (2002) found that among early career police officers, the organizational stressors measured as daily hassles in the work environment were directly related to PTSD symptoms. When considering the interpretation of these direct effects, it is necessary to realize that the symptoms of PTSD, such as intrusive memories of the event or suppression of thoughts about the event, are only experienced in relation to the specific experience of a traumatic event. Accordingly, in this study and others reported above, the findings suggest that the daily organizational stressors are acting to moderate the relationship between the experience of a traumatic event and PTSD symptoms. If those officers who experience operational stressors that are traumatic are also exposed to daily workplace hassles, then they are apparently more likely to develop PTSD symptoms. In the Huddleston study it is alarming to observe that at only six months into the police officers' careers, organizational stressors may already be predisposing some toward the development of a major disorder. Although there is much ongoing work to be done in this area, the available evidence already suggests that ongoing stressors and daily hassles and uplifts in the workplace must be taken seriously as an important aspect of the recovery from traumatic stress and the prevention of psychological disorder.

In considering the elements of an integrated response and providing an effective recovery environment following trauma, this chapter has laid some emphasis on the social and organizational environments. As researchers continue to study the different aspects of work-related trauma, and the development of PTSD by those at risk following traumatic stress at work, they are producing evidence suggesting that the social environment and organizational stressors in the workplace assume particular importance. It is apparent that social support at work from peers and supervisors, appropriate workplace attitudes toward talking about traumatic experience, and relief from routine or daily work stressors should be a major focus of preventive efforts. The organizational factors that have been consistently reported in relation to health outcomes are within the areas of workload, resources, and supervisory issues. The development of a healthy, positive, and supportive working environment in these terms is already accepted as a worthwhile aim for any organization due to a range of likely positive outcomes such as productivity and job satisfaction. Therefore, it seems unlikely that such an aim will be regarded as detrimental in the future. Rather, the development of a good working environment must be seen as a very positive focus for the resources and efforts that are directed toward the prevention of PTSD.

QUESTIONS FOR DISCUSSION

1. Discuss situations in which talking about work-related stressors is detrimental to recovery.
2. What is the role of social support on coping with PTSD?
3. In what ways does the organizational environment contribute to trauma recovery?
4. Discuss the various police experiences that contribute to PTSD among police officers.
5. Discuss psychological debriefing and its effectiveness at preventing PTSD.

REFERENCES

Alexander, D. A. (1993). Stress among police body handlers: A long-term follow-up. *British Journal of Psychiatry*, 163, 806–808.
Alexander, D. A. & Wells, A. (1991). Reactions of police officers to body-handling after a major disaster: A before-and-after comparison. *British Journal of Psychiatry*, 159, 547–555.
American Psychiatric Association. (1994). *Diagnostic and Statistical Manual of Mental Disorders* (4th ed.). Washington, DC: American Psychiatric Association.

Barnes, M. K. & Duck, S. (1994). Everyday communicative contexts for social support. In B. R. Burleson, T. L. Albrecht, & I. G. Sarason (Eds.), *Communication of Social Support. Messages, Interactions, Relationships, and Community* (pp. 175–194). Thousand Oaks, CA: Sage.

Bartone, P. T. (2000). Hardiness as a resiliency factor for U.S. forces in the Gulf War. In J. M. Violanti, D. Paton, & C. Dunning (Eds.), *Posttraumatic Stress Intervention: Challenges, Issues and Perspectives* (pp. 115–133). Springfield, IL: Charles C Thomas.

Best, S. R., Brunet, A., Weiss, D. S., Metzler, T., Rogers, C. E., Rosario, M., Fagan, J., & Marmar, C. R. (2000). Critical incident exposure and routine work stress in policing: Risk and resilience factors for posttraumatic stress reactions and emotional distress. Paper presented at the Third World Conference of the International Society for Traumatic Stress Studies, Melbourne, Australia.

Bisson, J. I. & Deahl, M. P. (1994). Psychological debriefing and prevention of post-traumatic stress: More research is needed. *British Journal of Psychiatry*, 165, 717–720.

Bootzin, R. R. (1997). Examining the theory and clinical utility of writing about emotional experiences. *Psychological Science*, 8, 167–169.

Boscarino, J. A. (1995). Post-traumatic stress and associated disorders among Vietnam veterans: The significance of combat exposure and social support. *Journal of Traumatic Stress*, 8, 317–336.

Brom, D., Kleber, R. J., & Hofman, M. C. (1993). Victims of traffic accidents: Incidence and prevention of post-traumatic stress disorder. *Journal of Clinical Psychology*, 49, 131–140.

Brown, J. M. & Campbell, E. A. (1990). Sources of occupational stress in the police. *Work and Stress*, 4, 305–318.

Carlier, I. V. E. (1999). Finding meaning in police traumas. In J. M. Violanti & D. Paton (Eds.), *Police Trauma: Psychological Aftermath of Civilian Combat* (pp. 227–240). Springfield, IL: Charles C Thomas.

Cohen, S. & Wills, T. A. (1985). Stress, social support, and the buffering hypothesis. *Psychological Bulletin*, 98, 310–357.

Deahl, M. P., Gillham, A. B., Thomas, J., Searle, M. M., & Srinivasan, M. (1994). Psychological sequelae following the Gulf War: Factors associated with subsequent morbidity and the effectiveness of psychological debriefing. *British Journal of Psychiatry*, 165, 60–65.

Dunning, C. (1999). Postintervention strategies to reduce police trauma: A paradigm shift. In J. M. Violanti & D. Paton (Eds.), *Police Trauma: Psychological Aftermath of Civilian Combat* (pp. 269–289). Springfield, IL: Charles C Thomas.

Evans, B. J. & Coman, G. J. (1993). General versus specific measures of occupational stress: An Australian police survey. *Stress Medicine*, 9, 11–20.

Evans, B. J., Coman, G. J., & Stanley, R. O. (1992). The police personality: Type A behavior and trait anxiety. *Journal of Criminal Justice*, 20, 429–441.

Everly, G. S. Jr., Boyle, S. H., & Lating, S. M. (1999). The effectiveness of psychological debriefing with vicarious trauma: A meta-analysis. *Stress Medicine*, 15, 229–233.

Fenlason, K. J. & Beehr, T. A. (1994). Social support and occupational stress: Effects of talking to others. *Journal of Organizational Behavior*, 15, 157–175.

Gersons, B. P. R. (1989). Patterns of PTSD among police officers following shooting incidents: A two-dimensional model and treatment implications. *Journal of Traumatic Stress*, 2, 247–257.

Green, B. L. (1994). Psychosocial research in traumatic stress: An update. *Journal of Traumatic Stress*, 7, 341–362.

Greenberg, M. A. (1995). Cognitive processing of traumas: The role of intrusive thoughts and reappraisals. *Journal of Applied Social Psychology*, 25, 1262–1296.

Griffiths, J. A. & Watts, R. (1992). *The Kempsey and Grafton Bus Crashes: The Aftermath.* Lismore, New South Wales, Australia: Instructional Design Solutions.

Hart, P. M., Wearing, A. J., & Headey, B. (1995). Police stress and well-being: Integrating personality, coping and daily work experiences. *Journal of Occupational and Organizational Psychology*, 68, 133–156.

Harvey, M. R. (1996). An ecological view of psychological trauma and trauma recovery. *Journal of Traumatic Stress*, 9, 3–23.

Horowitz, M. J. (1993). Stress-response syndromes: A review of posttraumatic stress and adjustment disorders. In J. P. Wilson and B. Raphael (Eds.), *International Handbook of Traumatic Stress Syndromes*. New York: Plenum.

Huddleston, L. (2002). The impact of traumatic and organizational stressors of New Zealand Police recruits: A longitudinal investigation of psychological health and posttraumatic growth outcomes. (Doctoral dissertation, Massey University, Palmerston North, New Zealand.)

Hytten, K. & Hasle, A. (1989). Fire fighters: A study of stress and coping. *Acta Psychiatrica Scandinavica*, 355 (suppl.), 50–55.

Kaufmann, G. M. & Beehr, T. A. (1989). Occupational stressors, individual strains, and social supports among police officers. *Human Relations*, 42, 185–197.

Kenardy, J. A., Webster, R. A., Lewin, T. J., Carr, V. J., Hazell, P. L., & Carter, G. I. (1996). Stress debriefing and the pattern of recovery following a natural disaster. *Journal of Traumatic Stress*, 8, 37–50.

Mann, J. P. & Neece, J. (1990). Workers' compensation for law enforcement related post traumatic stress disorder. *Behavioral Sciences and the Law*, 8, 447–456.

Manolias, M. B. & Hyatt-Williams, A. (1993). Effects of postshooting experiences on police-authorized firearms officers in the United Kingdom. In J. P. Wilson & B. Raphael (Eds.), *International Handbook of Traumatic Stress Syndromes*. New York: Plenum.

McFarlane, A. C. (1988). The longitudinal course of posttraumatic morbidity: The range of outcomes and their predictors. *The Journal of Nervous and Mental Disease*, 176, 30–39.

McFarlane, A. C., Atchison, M., Rafalowicz, E., & Papay, P. (1994). Physical symptoms in post-traumatic stress disorder. *Journal of Psychosomatic Research*, 38, 715–726.

Miller, I. (1996). Demography and attrition in the New Zealand Police 1985–95. Unpublished report: New Zealand Police National Headquarters.

Moran, C. & Britton, N. R. (1994). Emergency work experience and reactions to traumatic incidents. *Journal of Traumatic Stress*, 7, 575–585.

Norman, E. M. (1988). Post-traumatic stress disorder in military nurses who served in Vietnam during the war years 1965–1973. *Military Medicine*, 154, 238–242.

Norris, F. H. (1992). Epidemiology of trauma: Frequency and impact of different potentially traumatic events on different demographic groups. *Journal of Consulting and Clinical Psychology*, 60, 409–418.

Paton, D. (1997). *Dealing with Traumatic Issues in the Workplace* (3rd ed.). Coolum Beach, Australia: Gull Publishing.

Paton, D., Smith, L. M., Ramsay, R., & Akande, D. (1999). Assessing the impact of trauma in work-related populations: Occupational and cultural determinants of reactivity. In R. Gist & B. Lubin (Eds.), *Response to Disaster: Psychosocial, Community and Ecological Approaches* (pp. 83–99). Philadelphia: Brunner/Mazel.

Pogrebin, M. R. & Poole, E. D. (1991). Police and tragic events: The management of emotions. *Journal of Criminal Justice*, 19, 395–403.

Raphael, B., Meldrum, L., & McFarlane, A. C. (1995). Does debriefing after trauma work? *British Medical Journal*, 310, 1479–1480.

Shalev, A. Y. (1994). Debriefing following traumatic exposure. In R. J. Ursano, B. G. McCaughey & C. Fullerton (Eds.), *Individual and Community Responses to Trauma and Disaster* (pp. 201–219). Cambridge, UK: Cambridge University Press.

despite their tendency to turn to other Caucasian officers, do not label it as "forming bonds with whom one shares a racial bond." Thus, when Caucasian officers report higher levels of co-worker camaraderie than African Americans, the phenomenon may be the same as the latter's turning to members of their own racial group.

TRANSACTIONAL MODEL OF THE POLICE STRESS-COPING PROCESS

Looking only at the stressors endemic to police work and alternative methods for coping with them, most contemporary researchers who study police coping with stress test the transactional model advanced by Lazarus (1968, 1991) and his colleagues (Lazarus & Folkman, 1984; see also Aldwin, 1994; Band & Manuele, 1987). The fundamental proposition of the transactional model presents *threat appraisal* as a mediator between a person's objective experience of a potential stressor and that person's level of stress. This proposition is that "stress is not a property of the person, or of the environment, but arises when there is conjunction between a particular kind of environment and a particular kind of person that leads to a threat appraisal" (Lazarus, 1991, p. 3). Anshel (2000) recently adapted the transactional model of the stress process to explain the stress-coping process in police work.

Breaking from prior depictions of objective stressors being responded to with alternative, more or less effective coping approaches, Anshel's (2000) model incorporated distinct steps in coping. The model begins with the police officer detecting an encounter, event, or stimulus. Next, as part of *primary appraisal* (Lazarus, 1994), the officer evaluates the significance of the encounter. If an encounter or event is perceived as irrelevant, benign, or positive, it is not stressful and does not require coping. If, however, an officer cognitively appraises an encounter or event as either currently or potentially threatening, harmful, or challenging, it is stressful and requires coping. Thus, the officer's cognitive appraisal strongly influences her or his perception of the stressor's intensity and importance and, subsequently, the chosen coping strategy (Anshel, 2000, p. 383). At this point, the police officer engages in a *secondary appraisal* process of considering the available coping options for altering the perceived harm, threat, or challenge (Anshel, 2000; see also Lazarus, 1984; Lazarus & Folkman, 1984).

In the transactional model, in addition to the effect of the primary and secondary appraisals on coping (Lazarus, 1984), choice of coping strategy is further determined by the amount of personal control an officer believes she or he has over the stressful situation. "[P]ersonal control reflects an individual's belief, at a given point in time, in his or her ability to effect change in a desired direction on the environment" (Greenberger & Strasser 1986, p. 165). *Approach coping strategies* are typically used when an officer experiences or has to process intense, unpleasant, and/or threatening information. The objective of approach coping is "to control, to improve understanding, or to foster resourcefulness in dealing with sources of stress through either *approach-cognitive coping* (i.e., thoughts) or *approach-behavioral coping* (i.e., actions)" (italics added) (Anshel, 2000, p. 387; see also, Krohne, 1996). *Approach-behavioral coping* is typically used after an officer interprets an encounter or event as highly stressful, yet controllable (e.g., in response to a threat and/or challenge), and it involves "reducing a stressful situation by physically interacting with or confronting the source of stress for the purpose of controlling the situation" (Anshel, 2000, p. 388). Examples of approach-behavioral coping include obtaining information from or questioning a person, communicating feelings to others, making direct eye contact, giving verbal or written commands or instructions, confronting or restraining others physically, drawing a weapon, attempting to catch a suspect, or making an arrest. The other type of approach coping strategy, approach-cognitive coping, consists of using one's thoughts to manage, empower, or improve one's resources in dealing with perceived stress, for example, analyzing, planning, rehearsing, imaging, psyching up, reinterpreting or reappraising, rationalizing, and praying (Anshel, 2000, p. 388; Lazarus & Folkman, 1984).

In contrast to approach coping strategies, *avoidance coping strategies* are used by officers when the situation is uncontrollable, the officer's emotional resources are limited (e.g., low self-confidence, reduced energy), the source of stress is unclear or unknown, and/or there is little chance of resolving the situation. Avoidance coping strategies reflect "a conscious attempt to turn away or distract oneself from the source of stress, either cognitively or physically; to replace unpleasant, unconstructive thoughts with more positive self-talk; or to take the necessary time to enhance one's personal mental and physical resources and to think through a rational, logical, and effective reaction to the stressful situation" (Anshel, 2000, p. 389; see also Krohne, 1996; Roth & Cohen, 1986; Suls & Fletcher, 1985). Anshel further subdivides avoidance coping into *avoidance-cognitive coping* and *avoidance-behavioral coping*. Avoidance-cognitive coping consists of "thoughts that serve to distract, filter out or ignore, discount, or psychologically distance oneself from the source of stress" (Anshel, 2000, p. 390). Avoidance-behavioral coping is the actual actions an officer takes to physically remove him- or herself from the source of stress, which in turn serves to reduce or eliminate thoughts related to the stressor. Anshel contends that avoidance-behavioral coping can be either adaptive (e.g., exercise, avoiding an individual or situation, or moving ahead to the next task) or maladaptive (e.g., drug and/or alcohol use or abuse and overeating, all of which distract the individual from thinking about or dealing with the stressor). According to the model, although avoidance coping strategies may help officers in the short term to mentally escape from the unpleasant aftereffects of a stressful event, over the long term they are often less effective than mentally or physically confronting the source of stress (Anshel, 2000; see also Biggam et al., 1997; Dietrich, 1989; Lord et al., 1991; Violanti et al., 1985; Violanti et al., 1986; Walker, 1997).

For Anshel (2000) and Lazarus and Folkman (1984), coping outcomes are partially dependent upon the "goodness of fit" between the cognitive appraisal and the coping strategy. For instance, police officers who use maladaptive coping strategies or fail to accurately interpret and rationally react to work-related events or situations will experience chronic, long-term stress (see also Hurrell, 1995; Nordlicht, 1979). Also, failure to quickly and effectively cope with repeated attacks of verbal or sexual harassment, especially by a supervisor, colleague, or other individual with whom an officer is required to interact regularly, will most likely result in chronic stress (Anshel, 2000; see also Hart et al., 1995).

ALTERNATIVES TO THE TRANSACTIONAL MODEL

The transactional model provides a complex taxonomy of coping responses and recognizes that a person's thoughts during the appraisal process affect the choice of response. The model, however, pays scant attention to emotions, which when they are very strong and very negative are often what are on a stressed person's mind, nor does it explicitly incorporate any information on the structures of inequality that characterize police organizations and the larger society. Finally, Anshel's (2000) model presents an ending point at *secondary* appraisal, though it is certainly conceivable that after a person tries some type of coping, there is an assessment of the result, followed by new emotions and trying a different way of coping. The last part of the more completely delineated process has been called the *reappraisal process*, which Perrewe and Zellars (1999, p. 741) describe as:

> [t]he feedback process, wherein changes in both primary and secondary appraisals are brought about via individual reactions/coping and the environmental counter-reactions. These reactions and counter-reactions are appraised by the individual, leading to reappraisals of the person-environment relationships.

Anschel's exclusion of any consideration of power structures and differentials (including inequity and bias), and the potential for coping approaches that challenge these differentials, leads to his startling conclusions about coping with sexual harassment as a source of stress. He draws on Brown and Campbell's (1994) work to suggest that female officers should use avoidance coping in response to sexual harassment. In particular, he promotes the use of detachment (e.g., minimizing the situation, not taking it seriously), denial (e.g., trying not to notice), and relabeling or reappraisal (e.g., interpreting the behavior as a compliment) by female officers to cope with sexual harassment (Anshel, 2000). Not only does the promotion of these coping strategies contradict Anshel's previously described point that these forms of coping would lead to more long-term stress and burnout for female officers, but they also suggest that challenging gender-related abuse is not a viable coping approach.

Anschel did not, of course, completely deny the part played by emotion and social (or organizational) inequality in stress and coping. As noted above, he recognized that the amount of control a person thinks she or he has over a situation affects that person's choice of coping approach; we would add that perceptions of control are related to perceived and actual power differentials. He also noted that when a person's emotional resources are limited, she or he tends to use an avoidance coping strategy. More generally, the transactional model includes the proposition that specific appraisal patterns lead to negative emotions, such as anxiety or depression (Lazarus, 1990), and that having more coping options results in less stress and negative emotion (Fox, Dwyer, & Ganster, 1993; Landsbergis, 1988; Spector, 1987). However, neither emotion nor control and its link to power are given a central place as influences on the choice of coping approach. This choice is of central interest, both theoretically and practically, because, as we argued above, it can have more to do with the desirability of the outcome of stress for both the individual and the organization than does the initial stressor.

THE CENTRALITY OF EMOTIONS IN THE POLICE STRESS-COPING PROCESS

In recent years, some industrial and organizational psychologists (Fisher & Ashkanasy, 2000; Lewis & Haviland, 1993; Muchinsky, 2000) have had a growing interest in emotions as they relate to what is typically referred to as the organizational *stress-coping process*. This interest has been legitimized, in part, by the development of new techniques for measuring emotions, new ways of conceptualizing behavior and feelings, and an increased recognition of the importance of both cognition and emotion as influences on how people cope with workplace stress (see Lewis & Haviland, 1993; Perrewe & Zellars, 1999). Emotions, along with the causes that a person attributes to a potential stressor, can mediate the connection of a particular event to a person's secondary appraisal of coping choices. Thus, police officers who encounter the same potential stressor can react very differently, depending on the cause they attribute to the stressor and their own resulting emotions. For example, an interpretation of a sergeant's behavior as intended to damage an officer's career rather than evidence of the sergeant's lack of social graces would likely promote a more negative emotional response. Furthermore, an officer is most likely to be concerned with coping with those stressors that cause a significant and ongoing emotional response. In general, the meaning that an officer gives to an event and the emotion it evokes may be a much more important influence on the choice of coping response than the actual occurrence and nature of an event (Perrewe & Zellars, 1999). Therefore, the de-emphasis in theory and research on understanding emotions in relation to how police cope with stress is problematic (Perrewe & Zellars, 1999; see also Dewe, 1989).

Despite the requirement that police officers express, manage, mediate, confront, and control emotions and feelings as part of their daily work, the literature on policing has largely neglected emotions, including the connection of emotional labor to stress, and the degree to which emotions mediate the relationship between a stressor and the *secondary appraisal*. Police officers experience a wide range of workplace problems, events, and situations that trigger negative emotions as part of the process leading to workplace stress. Although the subject of police stress and coping has placed researchers "squarely into the arena of workplace emotions" (e.g., frustration, irritation, pain, guilt, fear, anger, despair, depression, and excitement), mainstream police scholars have never really allowed emotions to formally enter into the study of police stress and coping strategies (Muchinsky, 2000, p. 803; see also Martin, 1999; Violanti, 1981). Instead, police scholars often focus their research on cognitive explanations.

One explanation for police scholars' neglect of emotions is that police organizations and officers do not emphasize them, and in fact, there is much support in the organization for hiding emotions. Police agencies have adopted a professional model of police officers as logical, rational, and reasoned decision makers and mediators who fight crime and maintain order. Emotions are regarded as unwanted influences that deflect police officers from the path of objectivity and professionalism, as forces to be controlled and hidden by police officers, if not eliminated through training, socialization, and supervisory practices (see Martin, 1999; Violanti, 1981; Whyte, 1956). Police recruits in the academy are taught that professional behavior and demeanor entail the repression of emotional displays, and thus they should respond to dangerous situations in ways that impair emotional identification and reaction (Martin, 1999). Instructors often communicate this norm to police recruits through a combination of war stories and scenario training that emphasize the importance of solidarity, teamwork, toughness, and stoicism when confronted with pain, fear, anger, and tragedy. Throughout an officer's career, the occupational cultural belief that displaying or communicating emotions while performing police duties is a weakness is repeatedly communicated to police officers (see also Pogrebin & Poole, 1995).

To be "emotional" in police work reflects a tendency for weakness and femininity, unwanted and undesirable characteristics in an occupation that is traditionally seen as masculine in nature (Martin, 1999; Miller, 2000). The stereotypical masculine value system of the police culture emphasizes a preference for cold rationality, which is cultivated through a norm of emotional suppression and self-management (Martin, 1999; Violanti, 1981; see also Muchinsky, 2000). Thus, officers who display too much sympathy, despair, anger, or other emotion in dealing with pain, fear, danger, and tragedy while on the job are often viewed as unable to withstand the pressures of police work (Martin, 1999). Opportunities for venting and expressing emotions are typically limited to the backstage areas of the workplace (e.g., locker room) and occur off duty, in the privacy of one's home, during the course of informal social activities (e.g., over a drink at the bar), or in the presence of select members of one's family or work group (Martin, 1999, p. 114; see also Manning, 1997).

One of the few acceptable ways to show emotions, both on the front and back stages of the workplace, is through humor. According to Martin (1999, p. 123), humor is used by police officers "to vent feelings and emotions, avoid the impression of vulnerability, and lessen the harshness of a tragic experience." Moreover, the process of joking about tragic events and embarrassing situations offers police officers both a way to express emotions without damaging their professional image and to collectively empathize with each other's feelings and translate an individual experience into a group experience (Martin, 1999; also see Howard, Tuffin, & Stephens, 2000, p. 310).

An interesting study, though with possibly limited generalizability, is a discourse analysis of interviews with 12 New Zealand police (Howard et al., 2000). The authors found a *discourse of unspeakability*, in which officers described emotions as threatening to performance and therefore demanding management and control. They also discovered a *discourse of emotional disclosure*, in which officers presented themselves as culturally competent in understanding the need to disclose their emotional response to trauma. Most officers alternated between discourses depending on the context. Police engaged in *discourse of unspeakability* when they talked about revealing their own emotions, thereby preserving their own status and position. Talking about what others do, they presented themselves and their organizations as in sync with the cultural norm that people should openly disclose disturbing emotions.

In the rare instances that police scholars do discuss emotions, they often see them as the outcome of a cognitive evaluation process, a view advanced in Lazarus's transaction model. For instance, Violanti's (1981) early work on police stress and coping touched on the concept of emotions in the workplace in an examination of the relationship between depersonalization (i.e., the demand that officers standardize emotions in external interactions) and stress. He found that depersonalization showed a strong positive relationship to stress, suggesting an incongruity between real emotion and what is demanded by the organization. Still, Violanti and his colleagues have viewed emotion as primarily an affective response to a cognitive activity that generates meaning for an individual; in their view, stress is a cognitive response to a stressful encounter. For the past 20 years, he and other police scholars, like many industrial/organizational psychologists, have tended to pay little or no attention to the emotional component of job stress, but rather have "felt compelled to deflect our understanding away from these emotions into something that more readily fits with the prevailing organizational literature base, a literature based upon cognitions" (Muchinsky, 2000, p. 803).

Despite the recognition that humor and alternative discourses provide a glimpse into police officers' emotions, by and large people who are not police are not privy to their emotional response to a host of workplace stressors, some of which are and others of which are not related to police work. The result is that most people who study police give little attention to emotions.

The study of emotions in the police stress-coping process does not require police scholars to create a new scientific literature because useful theories and methods already exist in the industrial/organizational psychology literature (Muchinsky, 2000). For instance, Plutchik (1993) offers a theoretical model that incorporates both cognitive and emotional aspects of a person's response to stressors into the organizational stress-coping process. The model begins with a stimulus (e.g., a single event or series of events), which triggers an emotion, and then the emotion disrupts the stability of an individual at a given moment and/or over time and ultimately causes stress. Plutchik contends that most of the elements in the sequential chain are not available to consciousness because individuals typically do not know why they become emotional and do not recognize the functions served by their emotions. However, it is emotions that can imply the need for action and shape one's reactions to a situation. Thus, emotions should become a measuring point for stress rather than the event itself. After experiencing emotions, people typically begin the process of coping, and the coping action taken may or may not return the individual from the state of discomfort or emergency to the neutral or normal state (see also Muchinsky, 2000). In this model, the most important functions of coping are to regulate or manage stressful emotions (emotion-focused coping) and alter or manage the troubling situation that provoked the emotions and caused distress (problem-solving coping). In turn, the coping action taken further shapes one's emotions.

THE CENTRALITY OF UNEQUAL POWER IN THE POLICE STRESS-COPING PROCESS

Some organizational psychologists have criticized their colleagues who give appraisals and emotions prominence. Schaubroeck (1999) argued that inserting these constructs between objective stressors and the resulting stress and attempts at coping de-emphasizes the very thing that organizational psychologists should pay attention to: objective workplace conditions that need changing in order to reduce employee stress. He also pointed to their inattention to the construct of job control, which has a demonstrated effect on stress (e.g., Fox et al., 1993). In his view, models that give prominence to attributions of the cause of stressors and resulting emotions (i.e., the model advanced by Perrewe & Zellar) suggest strategies that will try to change individuals rather than organizations. Similarly, Frese and Zapf (1999, p. 762) argued for continued study of objective stressors and the state of organizations with the reasoning that if "stress were idiosyncratic and just related to an individual's perception or cognitive appraisals, it would not make sense to redesign working conditions. The only sensible approach would be to change the individual."

A singular focus on attribution and emotions can implicitly pathologize employees and devalue coping approaches that challenge and change police departments or result in escape from them (e.g., leaving the job). Although researchers and practitioners often present women's and minorities' attrition from police organizations as a personal failure in coping, the loss for the police department may be a triumph for the individual. As an example, many women and minorities have left policing for the less hostile atmosphere provided in some corporate security settings, thereby dramatically increasing their earnings and the fit between their range of abilities and the demands of the job. Based on clinical data from therapy with officers who were under such stress that they were considering leaving the force, Dick (2000) described "epiphanal events" that for some officers resulted in emotional exhaustion (i.e., burnout). At the epiphanal event, the officers reasoned that the organization stood in the way of their making their desired positive contribution through work. Dick presents this as evidence of an individual not coping in a way that allows continuation of work, but it can just as easily be seen as evidence of the inadequacies of police work and organizations.

A person's perceived social location (as a member of a gender, racial, ethnic, or other group) can impact her or his interpretation and related emotional response to an event. Seeing an event as part of a larger pattern of intentional bias would make it more meaningful and stressful. For example, if an officer in a racial or ethnic minority group interprets an event as biased, the result may be intense rage. A very different emotion would result if an officer interprets an event as an oversight. Also, officers who see themselves as powerless due to a disadvantaged social location will experience different emotions in the face of a stressor than those who feel they can effectively interrupt, change, or escape stressful situations, in other words, that they have power. People's sense of the relative power they have due to their social location influences their emotional response to a stressor.

ADVANCING THEORY, RESEARCH, AND PRACTICE RELEVANT TO THE STRESS-COPING PROCESS IN POLICE DEPARTMENTS

In the transactional model of police stress, cognitions mediate the connection of objective stressors in the workplace and an officer's choice of coping approach and how an officer copes with stress has an influence on her or his emotions. Yet our own discussion and the writing of organizational psychologists propose a considerably more complex model, most of which has been largely untested by research in any organization, let alone in police departments. Above, we have emphasized the centrality of emotions and of unequal power arrangements as necessary parts of theory to explain why a police officer copes with stressors in a particular way, and thus to explain the outcome of exposure to potential stressors. A consideration of emotions extends the model to include (1) how a person's attribution of the cause of the stressor affects feelings and (2) how a person interprets her or his own emotions. Emotions remain important in the recursive process of coping with stress, which includes assessment of how well sequential attempts at coping have worked. It is not only important to consider emotions but also to recognize that the effect of objective stressors is not totally eradicated by cognitive/emotional processing.

Fisher's (2000) recommendations for future study of the stress-coping process in a range of workplace settings apply to police. She argued for a move away from the nearly exclusive focus on cognitive evaluation of job features and for research that considers emotion (Fisher & Ashkanasy, 2000, p. 127). In this vein, one important question is, what role does emotional labor play in generating stress? The dominant view is that emotional labor is hard on people, especially for people who do not identify strongly with their job or their occupation and those who experience strong negative emotions (Schaubroeck & Jones, 2000).

Police are expected to display positive emotions in the station house and on the street. Widespread adoption of community policing and the focus on police-citizen relationships may increase the stringency of this requirement and the demands for emotional labor. What are the impacts on stress and coping? Steinberg (1999) has developed indexes of emotional labor and emotional demands, which could be used to understand whether some gender and minority groups or police occupied with community policing or other particular aspects of police work disproportionately are called on to do emotional labor. Findings about emotional labor, stress, and coping could shed light on why some police officers seek out certain assignments but others eschew them and why some but not other officers experience ill effects of stress.

At the same time that we establish the case for considering emotions in future research on police stress and coping, we recognize the challenge of doing this. Fisher (2000) used an innovative approach to measuring emotion of employees: *experience sampling methodology* (ESM) (Alliger & Williams, 1993; Hormuth, 1986; Larson & Csikszentmihalyi, 1983). ESM involved obtaining up to 50 reports of immediate mood and emotions from 121 employed persons over a two-week period. At each sampling, Fisher used her job emotions scale to tap a range of work-related positive emotions (liking for someone or something, happy, enthusiastic, pleased, proud, optimistic, enjoying something, and content) and negative emotions (depressed, frustrated, angry, disgusted, unhappy, disappointed, embarrassed, and worried). The rationale for using ESM is that moods and emotions are transient, making it difficult to measure them accurately. When people report retrospectively, they tend to inflate the frequency of both positive and negative emotions (Diener, Larsen, Levine, & Emmons 1985). Although the ESM and the job emotions scale solved the technical difficulty of measuring immediate emotion, applying them in a police setting would require the researcher to overcome the reticence of police about emotions and to have high levels of researcher-subject trust. Yet the approach may be selectively useful in settings with some degree of tolerance for researcher presence.

Dick (2000) concluded that clinical data provided access to the meanings that police gave to objective stressors and the reasoning surrounding the assignment of particular meanings. The clinical setting, and the immediate crisis that propelled police to seek help, can reduce barriers to discussion of emotion.

There are, however, drawbacks to using clinical data and, indeed, the theoretical framework that underpins the practice of cognitive therapy. Cognitive therapy is based on the notion that emotional disturbance results from irrational or illogical belief systems. However, emotional disturbance also can result when objective stressors exist in the first place, for instance, when evaluation practices are erratic or biased against some groups, adequate resources are not provided to accomplish job tasks, or the demands of shift work and of caring for young children just cannot be met with a person's existing resources. When a person does not have illogical belief systems, at the individual level the appropriate employee assistance is to provide support in changing, accepting, or leaving the place of work. At the organizational level, consistent with the discipline of organizational psychology, the task would be to redesign working conditions (Perrewe & Zellar, 1999, p. 750). Using clinical data for research can obscure the structure and practices of police departments at the same time that cognitive therapies might pathologize police who are responding quite reasonably to negative work environments.

Apart from methodological difficulties, the complexity of the elaborated (cognitions *and* emotions) and contextualized (power differentials inside and outside the police department) model of the stress-coping process requires measurement of several different constructs, or at least acknowledgment of the limitations of any research that omits one or more of them. First, various objective circumstances and events could be construed as stressors. Between this and the actual choice and use of some approach to coping are (1) appraisal of the event or circumstance as irrelevant, positive, or negative, (2) attribution of the cause of the stressor, (3) emotions that result from certain appraisals and attributions or directly from the existence of the stressor, (4) a consideration and choice of alternative coping response(s), (5) emotions that result from trying to cope in a certain way, (6) reappraisal of the situation, based in part on what happened after the police officer tried to cope in a certain way, followed by new emotions and new considerations of actions to use to cope. Whether this process is cut short (e.g., because the stressor evokes no emotional response) or continues, it occurs in a specific organizational and social structural context. The relevant context, which can influence appraisals, attributions, emotions, and choice of coping strategy, includes inequality both within and outside the department, police organizational culture and subgroup support (or discouragement) for the use of particular coping strategies, and the nature of potential stressors.

Much of what we have written about both theoretical and research challenges suggests the need for methodologies that place the researcher in close and continuous connection with police in their work environments. Observational, intensive interviewing and discourse analysis would be most useful in making sense of the relative salience of objective conditions, cognitions, emotions, coping approaches, and organizational context in leading to some particular positive or negative results for police and the way they do their job, or indeed, whether they find a new job. More quantitative methodologies, though, also would be useful in understanding modal emotional experiences (Schaubroeck, 1999), persistent patterns of causal attribution and appraisal, and common stressors that may add to understanding of the negative results of stress and ways that they can be minimized.

An expanded model of the process of stress and coping in police departments can be helpful in determining needed organizational changes. At the same time, it raises a caution about pathologizing the cognitions and emotions of people in organizations that expose employees to stress-producing circumstances and conditions or that limit (through norms or actions) the use of coping strategies. Dick (2000, p. 239) described the goals of emotive behavior therapy sessions for police who were experiencing stress: to establish the "(1) nature of the acute stressor; (2) current emotional state; (3) behaviors used to deal with the emotion; (4) the thoughts causing the emotion; and (5) the beliefs underlying the thoughts." Dick recognized that beliefs causing particular emotions were influenced by the broader police culture in the department. However, the solutions within this individual therapy approach did not extend to challenging the culture or changing the department. This may make sense in which one very stressful event, such as a physical attack, triggered thought processes that produced anxiety that persisted for a great length of time. However, anger and depression based on the assessment that the department prevented the police officer from doing a good job might indicate the need for organizational change. In fact, the cognitive therapy was most effective when there was anxiety triggered by reactions to one incident and it was least effective when officers felt anger and depression that they attributed to persisting department practices.

Since organization, cognition, and emotion are part of the stress-coping processes in police departments, there is merit to the idea of combining efforts to alter the job or aspects of police organizations and also teaching officers effective coping techniques (Hurrell, 1995). Particularly when sources of job-related stress are uncontrollable, training and therapy for individual police and preparation of police supervisors to encourage productive ways of understanding and bringing meaning to stressors and the emotions they evoke make sense (Anschel, 2000). However, to the extent that police organizational culture and the structure and practices of police departments create stressors, organizational change efforts would be most effective in the long run. Police organizational transformation is not widespread and is difficult (Morash & Ford, 2002), but it and other change strategies in policing need to be considered. Police subgroup support and advocacy groups, such as NOBLE (National Organization of Black Law Executives) and IAWP (International Association of Women Police), offer powerful group strategies for responding to stressors. The dual emphasis on improving the police stress-coping process by changing features of the police department and coping strategies of individuals can be informed by a parallel multilevel theory.

A multilevel theory would acknowledge emotions as well as cognition as legitimate domains of scientific inquiry in the study of police stress and coping and would not view emotions as simply the ancillary by-product of cognitive evaluations of a stressful event or annoyances that deflect people from objectivity (see Muchinsky, 2000; Perrewe & Zellars, 1999; Plutchik, 1993). In particular, there is a need to understand the different stressor-related emotions of police, their situation and structural sources, the interplay of emotions and cognitions, gender/race/ethnic and other group effects on felt, displayed, and expected emotions, the effect of emotions on officers' well-being, health and stress levels, and the role of emotions in shaping coping responses (Fisher & Ashkanasy, 2000).

At the same time that theory and practice attend to emotions, it is critical to know more about the concentration of some stressors on gender and minority police officers and of available resources used in alternative coping strategies. Without an understanding of emotions and the broader organizational context for policing, the discussion of coping strategies is incomplete.

QUESTIONS FOR DISCUSSION

1. What do police officers who experience high levels of occupational stress typically report as their symptoms?
2. In the transactional model of the stress-coping process, what is meant by the "threat appraisal"?
3. What does the officer do during the primary appraisal and secondary appraisal of the coping process?
4. After what type of experiences are approach coping strategies typically used by an officer?
5. Give some examples of avoidance-behavioral coping techniques that an officer might use.

REFERENCES

Aaron, J. (2000). Stress and coping in police officers. *Police Quarterly*, 3, 428–450.

Aldag, R. J. & Brief, A. P. (1979). Examination of a measure of higher-order need strength. *Human Relations*, 32, 705–718.

Aldwin, C. M. (1994). *Stress, Coping and Development*. New York: Guilford Press.

Aldwin, C. M. & Revenson, T. A. (1987). Does coping help? A reexamination of the relation between coping and mental health. *Journal of Personality and Social Psychology*, 53, 337–348.

Alexander, D. A. & Walker, L. G. (1994). A study of methods used by Scottish police officers to cope with work-induced stress. *Stress Medicine*, 10, 131–138.

Alkus, S. & Padesky, C. (1983). Special problems of police officers: Stress related issues and interventions. *Counseling Psychologist*, 11, 55–64.

Alliger, G. M. & Williams, K. J. (1993). Using signal-contingent experience sampling methodology to study work in the field: A discussion and illustration examining task perceptions and mood. *Personnel Psychology*, 46, 525–549.

Anshel, M. H. (2000). A conceptual model and implications for coping with stressful events in police work. *Criminal Justice and Behavior*, 27, 375–400.

Anshel, M. H., Robertson, M., & Caputi, P. (1997). Sources of acute stress and their appraisals and reappraisals among Australian police as a function of previous experience. *Journal of Occupation and Organizational Psychology*, 70, 337–356.

Band, S. R. & Manuele, C. A. (1987). Stress and police officer performance: An examination of effective coping behavior. *Journal of Police Criminal Psychology*, 3, 30–42.

Bannerman, E. D. (1997). Female police officers: The relationship between social support, interactional style, and occupational stress and strain. (Dissertation, Simon Fraser University, Vancouver, Canada.)

Banyard, V. L. & Graham-Bermann, S. A. (1993). Can women cope? A gender analysis of theories of coping with stress. *Psychology of Women Quarterly*, 17, 303–318.

Beehr, T. A., Johnson, L. B., & Nieva, R. (1995). Occupational stress: Coping of police and their spouses. *Journal of Organizational Behavior*, 16, 3–25.

Biggam, F. H., Power, K. G., & MacDonald, R. R. (1997). Self-perceived occupational stress and distress in a Scottish police force. *Work and Stress*, 11, 118–133.

Billings, A. G. & Moos, R. H. (1981). The role of coping responses and social resources in attenuating the stress of life events. *Journal of Behavioural Medicine*, 4, 139–157.

Brooks, L. W. & Piquero, N. L. (1998). Police stress: Does department size matter? *Policing: An International Journal of Police Strategies and Management*, 21, 600–617.

Brown, J. M. & Campbell, E. A. (1994). *Stress and Policing: Sources and Strategies.* New York: John Wiley & Sons.

Burke, R. J. (1998). Work and non-work stressors and well-being among police officers: The role of coping. *Anxiety, Stress and Coping*, 11, 345–362.

Burke, R. J. & Deszca, E. (1986). Correlates of psychological burnout phases among police officers. *Human Relations*, 39, 487–502.

Cullen, F. T., Lemming, T., Link, B. G., & Wozniak, J. F. (1985). The impact of social supports on police stress. *Criminology*, 3, 503–522.

Dewe, P. J. (1989). Examining the nature of work stress: Individual evaluations of stressful experiences and coping. *Human Relations*, 42, 993–1013.

Dick, P. (2000). The social construction of the meaning of acute stressors: A qualitative study of the personal accounts of police officers using a stress counseling service. *Work and Stress*, 14, 226–244.

Diener, E., Larsen, R. J., Levine, S., and Emmons, R. A. (1985). Intensity and frequency: Dimensions underlying positive and negative affect. *Journal of Personality & Social Psychology*, 48, 1253–1265.

Dietrich, J. (1989). Helping subordinates face stress. *Police Chief*, 56, 44–47.

Dietrich, J. & Smith, J. (1986). The nonmedical use of drugs including alcohol among police personnel: A critical literature review. *Journal of Police Science and Administration*, 14, 300–306.

Ellison, K. W. & Genz, J. L. (1978). The police officer as burned-out samaritan. *FBI Law Enforcement Bulletin*, 47, 1–7.

Etzion, D. & Pines, A. (1981). *Sex and Culture as Factors Explaining Reported Coping Behavior and Burnout of Human Service Professionals: A Social Psychological Perspective.* Tel Aviv: Tel Aviv University, the Israel Institute of Business Research.

Evans, B. J., Corman, G. J., Stanley, R. O., & Borrows, G. D. (1993). Police officers' coping strategies: An Australian police survey. *Stress Medicine*, 9, 237–246.

Fain, D. B. & McCormick, G. M. (1988). Use of coping mechanisms as a means of stress reduction in north Louisiana. *Journal of Police Science and Administration*, 16, 21–28.

Fisher, C. D. (2000). Mood and emotions while working: Missing pieces of job satisfaction? *Journal of Organizational Behavior*, 21, 185–202.

Fisher, C. D. & Ashkanasy, N. M. (2000). The emerging role of emotions in work life: An introduction. *Journal of Organizational Behavior*, 21, 123–129.

Fleishman, J. A. (1984). Personality characteristics and coping patterns. *Journal of Health and Social Behavior*, 25, 229–244.

Folkman, S. & Lazarus, R. S. (1980). An analysis of coping in a middle-aged community sample. *Journal of Health and Social Behavior*, 21, 219–239.

Folkman, S. & Lazarus, R. S. (1988). Coping as a mediator of emotion. *Journal of Personality and Social Psychology*, 50, 992–1003.

Fox, M. L., Dwyer, D. J., & Ganster, D. C. (1993). Effects of stressful job demands and control on physiological and attitudinal outcomes in a hospital setting. *Academy of Management Journal*, 36, 289–318.

Frese, M. & Zapf, D. (1999). On the importance of the objective environment in stress and attribution theory. Counterpoint to Perrewe and Zellars. *Journal of Organizational Behavior*, 20, 761–765.

Geick, E. (1998). Occupational stress of female police officers: An empirical investigation. (Dissertation, Texas A&M University.)

Golkasian, G. A., Geddes, R. W., & DeJong, W. (1985). *Coping with Police Stress*. Washington, DC: U.S. Government Printing Office.

Graf, F. A. (1986). The relationship between social support and occupational stress among police officers. *Journal of Police Science and Administration*, 14, 178–186.

Greenberger, D. B. & Strasser, S. (1986). Development and application of a model of personal control in organizations. *Academy of Management Review*, 11, 164–177.

Greenglass, E. R. (1995). Gender, work stress and coping: Theoretical implications. *Journal of Social Behavior and Personality*, 10, 121–134.

Haarr, R. N. & Morash, M. (1999). Gender, race, and strategies of coping with occupational stress in policing. *Justice Quarterly*, 16, 303–336.

Hart, P. M., Wearing, A. J., & Headey, B. (1995). Police stress and well-being: Integrating personality, coping and daily work experiences. *Journal of Occupational and Organizational Psychology*, 68, 133–156.

Hillgren, J. S., Bond, R., & Jones, S. (1976). Primary stressors in police administration and law enforcement. *Journal of Police Science and Administration*, 4, 445–449.

Hochschild, A. R. (1983). *The Managed Heart: Commercialization of Human Feeling*. Berkeley: University of California Press.

Holahan, C. J. & Moos, R. H. (1987). Personal and contextual determinants of coping strategies. *Journal of Personality and Social Psychology*, 52, 946–955.

Hormuth, S. E. (1986). The sampling of experiences in situ. *Journal of Personality*, 54, 262–293.

Howard, C., Tuffin, K., & Stephens, C. (2000). Unspeakable emotion: A discursive analysis of police talk about reactions to trauma. *Journal of Language & Social Psychology*, 19, 295–314.

Hurrell, J. J. Jr. (1995). Police work, occupational stress and individual coping. *Journal of Organizational Behavior*, 16, 27–28.

Kirkcaldy, B., Cooper, C. L., & Ruffalo, P. (1995). Work stress and health in a sample of U.S. police. *Psychological Reports*, 76, 700–702.

Kop, N., Euwema, M., & Schaufeli, W. (1999). Burnout, job stress, and violent behaviour among Dutch police officers. *Work and Stress*, 13, 326–340.

Kroes, W. H., Margolis, B. L., &. Hurrell, J. J. Jr. (1974). Job stress in policemen. *Journal of Police Science and Administration*, 2, 145–155.

Krohne, H. W. (1996). Individual differences in coping. In M. Zeidner & N. S. Endler (Eds.), *Handbook of Coping* (pp. 381–409). New York: John Wiley & Sons.

Landsbergis, P. A. (1988). Occupational stress among health care workers: A test of the job demands-control model. *Journal of Organizational Behavior*, 9, 217–239.

LaRocco, J. M., House, J. W., & French, J. R. P. Jr. (1980). Social support, occupational stress, and health. *Journal of Health and Social Behavior*, 21, 202–218.

Larson, R. & Csikszentmihalyi, M. (1983). The experience sampling method. *New Directions for Methodology of Social & Behavioral Science*, 15, 41–56.

Laufersweiler-Dwyer, D. L. & Dwyer, G. R. (2000). Profiling those impacted by organizational stressors at the macro, intermediate, and micro levels of several police agencies. *Justice Professional*, 12, 443–369.

Lazarus, R. S. (1968). Emotions and adaptation: Conceptual and empirical relations. *Nebraska Symposium on Motivation,* 16, 175–266.

Lazarus, R. S. (1984). On the primacy of cognition. *American Psychologist,* 39, 124–129.

Lazarus, R. S. (1990) Theory-based stress management. *Psychological Inquiry*, 1, 3–13.

Lazarus, R. S. (1991). *Emotion and Adaptation.* New York: Oxford University Press.

Lazarus, R. S. (1994). Psychological stress in the workplace. Handbook on Job Stress [Special Issue]. *Journal of Social Behavior and Personality*, 6, 1–13.

Lazarus, R. S. & Folkman, S. (1984). *Stress, Appraisal and Coping.* New York: Springer.

Lewis, M. & Haviland, J. M. (1993). Preface. In M. Lewis & J. M. Haviland (Eds.), *Handbook of Emotions.* New York: Guilford Press.

Lord, V. B. (1996). An impact of community policing: Reported stressors, social support, and strain among police officers in a changing police department. *Journal of Criminal Justice*, 24, 503–522.

Lord, V. B., Gray, D. O., & Pond, S. B. (1991). The Police Stress Inventory: Does it measure stress? *Journal of Criminal Justice*, 19, 139–149.

Lykes, M. B. (1983). Discrimination and coping in the lives of black women: Analyses of oral history data. *Journal of Social Issues*, 39, 79–100.

Malloy, T. E. & Mays, L. (1984). The police stress hypothesis: A critical evaluation. *Criminal Justice and Behavior*, 11, 197–224.

Manning, P. K. (1997). *Police work: The social organization of policing* (2nd ed.). Prospect Heights, IL: Waveland Press.

Martin, S. E. (1999). Police force or police service? Gender and emotional labor. *Annals, AAPSS*, 561, 111–126.

Miller, S. (2000). *Gender and community policing: Walking the talk.* Boston, MA: Northeastern University Press.

Moos, R. H. & Moos, B. S. (1984). The process of recovery from alcoholism: Comparing family functioning in alcoholic and matched control families. *Journal of Studies on Alcohol*, 45, 111–118.

Morash, M. & Ford, J. K. (2002). *Move to Community Policing: Making Change Happen.* Royal Oaks, CA: Sage.

Morash, M. & Haarr, R. N. (1995). Gender, workplace problems and stress in policing. *Justice Quarterly*, 12, 113–140.

Muchinsky, P. M. (2000). Emotions in the workplace: The neglect of organizational behavior. *Journal of Organizational Behavior*, 21, 801–806.

Neighbors, H. W., Jackson, J., Bowman, P., & Gurin, G. (1983). Stress, coping and black mental health: Preliminary findings from a national study. *Prevention in Human Services*, 2, 5–29.

Nordlicht, S. (1979). Effects of stress on the police officer and family. *New York State Journal of Medicine*, 79, 400–401.

Norvell, N., Belles, D., & Hills, H. (1988). Perceived stress levels and physical symptoms in supervisory law enforcement personnel. *Journal of Police Science and Administration*, 16, 75–79.

Paton, D. & Violanti, J. M. (1997). Long-term exposure to stress and trauma: Addiction and separation issues in police officers. In G. M. Habermann (Ed.), *Looking Back and Moving Forward: 50 Years of New Zealand Psychology* (pp. 194–201). Wellington, New Zealand: New Zealand Psychological Society.

Pearlin, L. & Schooler, C. (1978). The structure of coping. *Journal of Health and Social Behavior*, 19, 2–21.

Perrewe, P. L. & Zellars, K. L. (1999). An examination of attributions and emotions in the transactional approach to the organizational stress process. *Journal of Organizational Behavior*, 20, 739–752.

Plummer, D. L. & Slane, S. (1996). Patterns of coping in racially stressful situations. *Journal of Black Psychology*, 22, 302–315.

Plutchik, R. (1993). Emotions and their vicissitudes: Emotions and psychopathology. In M. Lewis & J. M. Haviland (Eds.), *Handbook of Emotions*. New York: Guilford Press.

Pogrebin, M. R. & Poole, E. D. (1995). Emotional management: A study of police response to tragic events. *Social Perspectives on Emotion* (Vol. 3). Greenwich, CT: JAI.

Roth, S. & Cohen, L. J. (1986). Approach, avoidance, and coping with stress. *American Psychologist*, 41, 813–819.

Schaubroeck, J. (1999). Should the subjective be the objective? On studying mental process, coping behavior, and actual exposures in organizational stress research. *Journal of Organizational Behavior*, 20, 753–760.

Schaubroeck J. & Jones, J. R. 2000. Antecedents of workplace emotional labor dimensions and moderators of their effects on physical symptoms. *Journal of Organizational Behavior*, 21, 163–183.

Sewell, J. D. (1981). Police stress. *FBI Law Enforcement Bulletin*, 50, 7–11.

Silbert, M. H. (1982). Job stress and burnout of new police officers. *Police Chief*, 49, 46–88.

Singleton, G. W. & Teahan, J. (1978). Effects of job-related stress on the physical and psychological adjustment of police officers. *Journal of Police Science and Administration*, 6, 355–361.

Smyth, K. A. & Williams, P. D. (1991). Patterns of coping in black working women. *Behavioral Medicine*, 17, 40–46.

Spector, P. E. (1987). Interactive effects of perceived control and job stressors on affective reactions and health outcomes for clerical workers. *Work and Stress*, 1, 155–162.

Spielberger, C. D., Westberry, L. G., Grier, K. S., & Greenfield, G. (1981). *Police stress survey: sources of stress in law enforcement*. Monograph Series 3, Number 6. Tampa, FL: University of South Florida, Human Resources Institute.

Steinberg, R. J. (1999). Emotional labor in job evaluation: Redesigning compensation practices. *Annals of the American Academy of Political and Social Science*, 561, 153–158.

Steinberg, R. J. & Figart, D. M. (1999). Emotional demands at work: A job content analysis. *Annals of the American Academy of Political and Social Science*, 561, 177–191.

Stephens, C., Long, N., & Miller, I. (1997). The impact of trauma and social support on posttraumatic stress disorder: A study of New Zealand police officers. *Journal of Criminal Justice*, 25, 303–314.

Stevenson, T. M. (1988). Stress among police officers: Burnout and its correlates. (Doctoral dissertation: California School of Professional Psychology.)

Storch, J. E. & Panzarella, R. (1996). Police stress: State-trait anxiety in relation to occupational and personal stressors. *Journal of Criminal Justice*, 24, 99–107.

Stotland, E. & Pendleton, M. (1989). Workload, stress, and strain among police officers. *Behavioral Medicine*, 15, 5–18.

Strentz, T. & Auerbach, S. M. (1988). Adjustment to the stress of simulated captivity: Effects of emotion-focused coping versus problem-focused preparation on hostages differing in locus of control. *Journal of Personality and Social Psychology*, 55, 652–660.

Stroman, C. A. & Seltzer, R. (1991). Racial differences in coping with job stress: A research note. *Journal of Social Behavior and Personality*, 6, 309–318.

Suls, J. & Fletcher, B. (1985). The relative efficacy of avoidant and nonavoidant coping strategies: A meta-analysis. *Health Psychology*, 4, 249–288.

Teahan, J. E. (1975). A longitudinal study of attitude shifts among black and white police officers. *Journal of Issues*, 31, 47–55.

Terry, W. C. (1985). Police stress as a professional self-image. *Journal of Criminal Justice*, 13, 501–512.

Violanti, J. M. (1981). Police stress and coping: An organizational analysis. (Doctoral dissertation, State University of New York at Buffalo.)

Violanti, J. M. (1992). Coping strategies among police recruits in a high-stress training environment. *Journal of Social Psychology*, 132, 717–729.

Violanti, J. M. (1993). What does high stress police training teach recruits? An analysis of coping. *Journal of Criminal Justice*, 21, 411–417.

Violanti, J. M. & Aron, F. (1993). Sources of police stressors, job attitudes and psychological distress. *Psychological Reports*, 72, 899–904.

Violanti, J. M. & Aron, F. (1994). Ranking police stressors. *Psychological Reports*, 75, 824–826.

Violanti, J. M. & Marshall, J. R. (1983). The police stress process. *Journal of Police Science and Administration*, 11, 389–394.

Violanti, J. M., Marshall, J. R., & Howe, B. (1985). Stress, coping, and alcohol use: The police connection. *Journal of Police Science and Administration*, 13, 106–110.

Violanti, J. M., Vena, J. E., & Marshall, J. R. (1986). Disease risk and mortality among police officers: New evidence and contributing factors. *Journal of Police Science and Administration*, 14, 17–23.

Walker, M. (1997). Conceptual and methodological issues in the investigation of occupational stress: A case study of police officers deployed on body recovery duty. *Policing and Society*, 7, 1–17.

Washington, B. (1981). Stress and the female officer. In L. Territo & H. J. Vetter (Eds.), *Stress and Police Personnel* (pp. 142–147). Needham Heights, MA: Allyn & Bacon.

Wexler, J. G. & Logan, D. D. (1983). Sources of stress among women police officers. *Journal of Police Science and Administration*, 11, 46–53.

Wharton, A. S. (1993). The affective consequences of service work: Managing emotions on the job. *Work & Occupations*, 20, 205–232.

Wharton, A. S. & Erickson, R. J. (1993). Managing Emotions on the Job and at Home: Understanding the consequences of multiple emotional roles. *Academy of Management Review*, 18, 457–486.

White, S. E. & Marino, K. E. (1983). Job attitudes and police stress: An exploration study of causation. *Journal of Police Science and Administration*, 11, 264–274.

Whyte, W. H. (1956). *The Organization Man*. New York: Simon & Schuster.

Wills, T. A. (1990). Social support and interpersonal relationships. In M. S. Clark (Ed.), *Review of Personality and Social Psychology* (pp. 265–289). Newbury Park, CA: Sage.

Worden, A. P. (1993). The attitudes of women and men in policing: Testing conventional and contemporary wisdom. *Criminology*, 31, 203–242.

11

Reflections on Policing and Stress

M. L. Dantzker

My interest in the relation between stress and policing began in the late 1980s while I was a full-time police officer working on my Ph.D. As a police officer with a college degree, a rarity in those days, I was extremely interested in the influence or effect education had on police performance. Of particular interest was its effect on perceptions of stress among police officers. The result was my dissertation, for which I examined officers' perceptions about the stressfulness of a variety of police-related stressors. My findings suggested that the relationship between education and perceptions of stress produced a roller-coaster effect; that is, officers with only a high school education had relatively high perceptions of stress while those with a bachelor's degree showed even higher levels. Individuals with a master's degree reported the lowest levels of perceived stress (Dantzker, 1998). Since these findings, little has been done to explore this relationship between stress and educational attainment.

Actually, as I read through all the chapters in this book, I realized that not much new has been written about stress since I completed my dissertation. A majority of the information provided in this text has not changed in the past 30 years, let alone the last 15. However, I have changed, to some degree, since my research in the late 1980s. In the early days I truly believed that policing was an extremely stressful occupation regardless of how much education or experience one possessed. Since those days, I have come to view policing as I would any occupation—that it has its stressful moments but in and of itself is no more stressful an occupation than any other. How it is viewed by the individual officer is what determines how stressful policing truly is.

Stress is confronted by all members of every occupation or profession known to society. The affect or impact of stress differs from individual to individual. What is extremely stressful to one individual may be only moderately stressful to another. The difference is nothing more than a matter of perception. Perception, according to *Webster's Dictionary,* is "consciousness; a result of perceiving; a mental image; awareness of the elements of the environment through physical sensation; physical sensation interpreted in the light of experience; quick, acute, and intuitive cognition; and a capacity for comprehension" (1988, p. 872).

Perception is a major element of social psychology. For social psychologists, it is important to understand "how people perceive each other, how they interpret other people's behavior, and how their attitudes form and change" (Sears, Peplau, Freedman, & Taylor, 1988, p. 6). It is from the social psychological perspective that stress is addressed in this closing chapter. The position offered is that while policing may be rife with *episodic* stressors, it is individual perceptions that determine just how stressful policing is to the individual rather than it being a stressful occupation, a position more widely supported throughout this book. Keep in mind this is merely one person's perception of stress and policing.

My career as a full-time police officer lasted from 1981 until 1987, when I went into academe full-time. For the past three years I have been a reserve deputy. In between, I made my fair share of ride-alongs across the country with officers from a variety of agencies, large and small, municipal and county. In total, I have more than 20 years of observations, wearing the uniform and from behind the uniform. My conclusion: policing is no more stressful an occupation than most. Actually, I have more stress as a college professor than as a police officer. The nights I go out on patrol are often more relaxing than my hours spent earlier in the day at the university. Why? My hypothesis about level of stress is that it is a matter of perception.

As previously noted, perceptions are based on how individuals accept or view an issue, item, situation, or problem, relying on personal beliefs, experiences, ideals, and so on, to form the perception. This often will result in no two people seeing something the same way. Thus my hypothesis regarding stress and policing is that no two police officers perceive a situation or problem the same way. Therefore, what is stressful to one officer may not be to another, or at least the levels of stressfulness will certainly differ.

The majority of the authors in this text tend to support the contention that policing is a stressful occupation and agencies must take measures to address stress among police officers. While I agree that policing can be very stressful, it depends on the individual, and agencies should have resources available to assist those who are quite capable of doing the job but, at times, may require assistance dealing with their perceptions of stressfulness. I'll now apply my position to the contents of this text.

Stevens sets the groundwork for the discussion of policing as a stressful occupation. He covers all the foundations found in the literature regarding police stress. Although he focuses on the police organizational structure and the effect it can have on police stress, the main focus is on the results of a study conducted before and after the terrorist attack on the World Trade Center on September 11, 2001. Of particular interest was whether perceptions of stress among police officers differed prior to and after the horrific event. Stevens found that post-9/11 perceptions of stress had intensified.

Based on my position, the findings should not be surprising. The events of September 11 were perhaps the most terrifying experiences that any person in this country may have had to deal with up to that point in his or her life. Police officers are no different. Although they may have experience dealing with highly stressful and horrific events (i.e., traffic fatalities, child abuse, murder), nothing could have prepared them for the death and destruction of

September 11. Is it any wonder that while dealing with loss of life and destruction at the level of September 11, police officers may have higher perceptions of stress? I would think not. However, how high those levels of stress may be could easily be attributed to individual perceptions. The fact is some officers will not deal with being a police officer as easily as they may have prior to September 11. Yet how they do deal with it will be strongly based on personal perceptions.

An excellent follow-up to Stevens's chapter is Paton's discussion in Chapter 2 on critical incidents. In this chapter, Paton looks at how critical incidents are linked with stress, particularly the long-term aspect of stress. He begins by looking at the origins of the critical incident stressors and how these experiences can be conceptualized as a series of phases, each with its own distinct set of potential stressors. Paton continues with a description of the critical incident response as being three phases: alarm and mobilization, response, and letdown and reintegration. A major phase is the response, which takes into account personal, cognitive, group, and organizational factors. As he notes, "the manner in which officers assimilate positive outcomes and resolve adverse outcomes associated with their critical incident involvement determines their future stress vulnerability and resilience." In other words, it's how officers *perceive* the critical incident and what they take away from it that can make a difference in how stressful other events may become.

Chapter 3 takes us in a slightly different direction, narrowing the focus from stress related to major critical incidents to a rather common event for most police officers, the domestic dispute. In this chapter, Van Wyk looked specifically at stress related to responding to a domestic dispute. She suggested that there are five social sources that could impact how the officer responds to the dispute: sexism, racism, dynamics of partner violence, normative perceptions of family and privacy, and media and publicity. Beginning with gender, Van Wyk advocates that gender produces stress for police officers via the cultural proscriptions for behavior, personality, and characteristics that ascribe value to male officers over female officers. That is, when a male and female officer respond to a dispute, this gender difference could produce stress in how they handle the situation, especially if the male officer has prescribed to certain gender-specific perceptions. Dealing with both a female partner and a female subject could be stressful for the officer. Race, too, according to Van Wyk, is a social construct that can increase the likelihood and prevalence of strain experienced by police officers. Whether within the police partnership or within the confines of the dispute, how the officer perceives individuals based on their race could be problematic.

Because family may be perceived as a private institution in which police interference/intervention should not occur, Van Wyk notes how this perception could cause stress for the officer. If his or her perceptions are that "this is a family matter," obviously having to interfere could cause strain for the officer.

Bad publicity is relatively common for policing. Regarding the media and publicity, Van Wyk indicates that if police officers perceive that how they handle a domestic dispute may receive negative publicity, it could cause them additional stress.

Finally, Van Wyk advises that the dynamics of the partnership could cause strain for a police officer. She suggested that police officers may have less stress when dealing with spousal disputes than any other type of partnership. Overall, Van Wyk's position tends to bolster the position that how the officer perceives the combatants and the given situation determines how much stress is attached to responding to a domestic dispute.

Staying with more specific stress-related situations, Lord in Chapter 4 looked at the stress of change. In particular, she examined organizational stressors resulting when a traditional policing approach changes to a community-oriented, problem-solving (COP) approach. Her study sought to identify three things:

1. The factors that the officers and their immediate supervisors actually considered stressful
2. The effectiveness of their social support systems to mediate the effects of stress
3. The effects stress was actually having on the officers

Lord identified a number of COP-related stressors: lack of recognition by the public, administration, and other officers; lack of communication between the different types of line officers and from supervisors; lack of participation in decisions; and role change specifically pertaining to the COP philosophy and practice. She found that change did relate significantly to stress. Again, the matter of perception comes into play. Obviously each officer will perceive the change differently, and thus, how stressful it becomes will be a matter of individuality.

The first four chapters focused on stress as it relates to events or change. The potential consequences of stress are addressed starting with Kerley in Chapter 5. In focusing on the main consequences, he divides them into three categories: on-the-job, physical and emotional, and family and relational. With respect to on-the-job consequences, two that Kerley noted are poor job performance and excessive use of force. Examples of physical and emotional consequences he gave were excessive drinking, use of drugs, and heart problems. A key family and relational consequence among police officers was identified as divorce. In all, Kerley noted that unrecognized and untreated stress has many consequences for both the officer and the agency. Furthermore, he suggested that there are many unanswered questions and a need for future discussion.

From my own perspective, I reiterate that the consequences may be very minimal for the officer, depending on how he or she perceives stress. Obviously the officer who dwells on the negative aspects will suffer worse consequences than the officer who deals with the issue and then moves on. Police agencies can help by offering officers a means for coping with stress-related problems without adding to their stress by making them think that there is something wrong with them experiencing stress when others may not.

Continuing with the consequences of stress, Violanti in Chapter 6 discusses the social-disease hypothesis as it applies to policing. His chapter continues where Kerley left off in looking at additional problems that can arise for police officers due to stress. His is the only other chapter in this text where I find explicit support for my position of "episodic stress." Violanti noted that "police work is usually routine in nature with episodic moments of intensive danger and stress." As he further noted, "police officers are not only exposed to a variety of stressors in their work, but also to a taxing 'routine' of boredom, interfaced with sporadic incidents of violence and at times life-and-death decisions."

While I do not like the use of "routine" to describe police activities because the fact is no two events are the same, there is often a routine to how officers may approach similar events (Dantzker, 2003). Following the routine helps limit how stressful an event is perceived as being. Still, it ultimately relies on the individual officer to perform and deal with police activities as best as he or she can. As Violanti pointed out, resiliency is an important individual trait.

Perhaps the worst consequence for a stressed police officer is suicide. In Chapter 7, Loo addresses this unfortunate outcome. He begins by suggesting that the reasons for police officers committing suicide include drug abuse, illness, marital and relationship problems, disciplinary and criminal action, personality characteristics, and dysfunction. Although there is a belief that there may be a high rate of suicide among police officers, Loo discusses the problems with suicide rates and theories of police suicide. His main focus is the establishment of a psychosocial process model to police suicide that begins with stressors followed by moderating variables, at which point the officer can partake in adaptive coping or suffer further stress reactions. Suffering further stress reactions and having the ready means to commit suicide (i.e., the service weapon) will lead to the suicide act.

Loo noted two key elements to this model that may prevent the suicide act: individual characteristics and social supports. Here again, the individual's perceptions play a key role. If the officer perceives that all is lost and there is no hope, then suicide is more imminent. To avoid reaching that point, preventive actions are necessary. Loo concludes by identifying a number of preventive actions which include stress management training, stress inoculation training, psychological services, and psychological assessments for special duties and critical incidents.

A question of interest is, how does gender affect perspective? Piquero offers insight in Chapter 8, where she examined stress from a gender perspective applying general strain theory. The chapter is based on a study she conducted that examined three questions:

1. Whether there are mean level differences in strain, negative emotions, and coping skills between male and female police officers.
2. Whether the strain-negative emotion relationship varies across gender.
3. Whether the theoretical process outlined by general strain theory operates in the same way across males and females in predicting violent abuse.

Her basic findings indicated that males were more likely to report stressors inherent to policing as well as media stress while females reported more female-specific stressors.

For females, Piquero found that job support and stress inherent to policing were significantly associated with anxiety, depression, and cynicism. Overall, her results offered mixed support for general strain theory. However, they did appear to offer concrete evidence that there is a perceptional difference by gender and that the perceptions do seem to have an effect on levels of stress.

Regardless of the officer's general demeanor, stress from a critical event is often unavoidable. How the officer responds to that stress may result in posttraumatic stress disorder (PTSD). Stephens, in Chapter 9, provided an outline of the causes and incidence of PTSD. She begins with identifying the kinds of events that may be traumatic, followed by a discussion of traumatic events that occur outside the workplace. In examining PTSD, Stephens suggested that the health effects of traumatic stress must be considered in an organizational context. Finally, she concludes her chapter with a discussion of preventive strategies that include psychological briefings, personal characteristics, social environment, and organizational factors. Although one event may cause severe PTSD for an officer, the same event may have little impact in another. As I have advocated throughout this chapter, perceptions are important to how stress is recognized and addressed.

Piquero offers insight regarding stress and gender. Her chapter receives support from Haarr and Morash in Chapter 10, in which the two looked at how emotions, gender, and minority status relate to coping and stress. They suggested that there is a need for a multilevel theory to explain coping that would acknowledge that emotions as well as cognition are legitimate domains of scientific inquiry in the study of police stress and coping. Citing Fisher and Ashkanasy (2000), Haar and Morash suggested that:

> [t]here is a need to understand the different stressor-related emotions of police, their situation and structural sources, the interplay of emotions and cognitions, gender/race/ethnicity and other group effects on felt, displayed, and expected emotions, the effect of emotions on officers' well-being, health and stress levels, and the role of emotions in shaping coping responses.

Emotions revolve around perceptions. Therefore, perceptions play an important role in how stress is perceived and in coping.

In closing, the question remains, is policing a stressful occupation? The answer most often would be yes, but then again so is almost any occupation for which individuals are required to respond to events or situations that may be perceived as stressful. It is that perception that influences just how stressful something is viewed as being, and that view plays a significant role in how an officer copes with the stress (Aaron, 2000). Does this mean that police agencies should continue to ignore the stress-related aspects of police work? No, but it does mean that agencies should consider taking an individual approach rather than a global approach. Reality dictates that some individuals will find police work more stressful than others. Either offer those individuals assistance or encourage them to find less stressful work. Perhaps they could become academics.

QUESTIONS FOR DISCUSSION

1. Based on the earlier reading, do you agree or disagree with Dantzker that policing is no more stressful than any other occupation? Why or why not?
2. What role do individual perceptions play in determining the level of stress officers experience while on the job?
3. Choose a chapter in the text and show how Dantzker's idea of perception can be used to reinterpret the findings.
4. Imagine you were assigned the task of reducing police stress and the consequences of it for your local police department. Using Dantzker's ideas, what policies would you implement?

REFERENCES

Aaron, J. D. K. (2000). Stress and coping in police officers. *Police Quarterly*, 3(4), 438–450.
Dantzker, M. L. (1998). The effect of education on police performance: The stress perspective. (Doctoral dissertation, University of Michigan.) Ann Arbor, MI: U.M.I. Dissertation Service.
Dantzker, M. L. (2003). *Understanding Today's Police* (3rd ed.). Upper Saddle River, NJ: Prentice Hall.
Sears, D. O., Peplau, L. A., Freedman, J. L., & Taylor, S. E. (1988). *Social Psychology* (6th ed.). Englewood Cliffs, NJ: Prentice Hall.
Webster's Ninth New Collegiate Dictionary (1988). Springfield, MA: Merriam-Webster Inc.